# THE TACOS AND CHOCOLATE DIET

# THE TACOS AND CHOCOLATE DIET

## HOW TO LIVE A BOLD, ADVENTUROUS, AND INTENTIONAL LIFE*

Drew Myers

Open Mouth Communications

# Preface

**\*Spoiler Alert: This is not a diet book. It's a book about taking action to live your best life.**

I have lived in Texas my whole life — except for when I took a job at a newspaper in southern Oregon for one year. I was twenty-three years old. I had moved to the West Coast a year after graduating from college, looking for that once-in-a-lifetime adventure. A friend of mine moved with me, and we were well on our way to living with reckless abandon.

Exactly 365 days later, I moved back to Texas. I told people I missed my mommy, which was accurate. My buddy stayed behind and boldly continued living the adventurous dream *(shout out to Chris)*. I returned home to live an adventure of a different kind.

There are memories and unforgettable experiences from my brief stint in Oregon, but none more life-changing than the slice of wisdom I received from a homeless man over a pint of beer.

We called him "Crazy Joe" for no other ignorant reason than we never asked him his name, and he often mumbled to himself. He lived on the streets of Ashland, Oregon, and cleaned up around several of the local bars to make money for food. I think part of his compensation was also free pints of that week's trendy microbrew. On many nights, he could be found drinking with the locals.

One slow night, I sat at the bar with Crazy Joe. We talked, and he introduced himself as Patrick. We were a few pints for the better, so his speech was slurred even more than usual as he talked about his life. Most of what he said was incoherent, and the beer had also put me in an amber haze. During one of his stories, however, his soft, raspy voice became crystal clear. I wish I could remember all the dialogue, but I don't. What I do remember, though, I've carried with me ever since.

Patrick looked me in the eye and said, "I don't want things to happen accidentally. I want things to happen on purpose."

It was as if he had cut into my soul with one phrase and burned it into my subconscious forever. He made me realize I was in charge of my destiny. I've held Patrick's philosophy close to my heart, and I've used his words to choose every path I took in my life since that moment.

Years later, I heard a wild story about Patrick taking out a pair of pliers and ripping a rotten tooth out of his mouth. It was likely he played dentist in the same bar he offered me his advice. While the story was a little disturbing — and gruesome — it didn't change the fact that this man had a profound impact on my life.

Even as I write this book, Patrick's whisper still inspires me.

– – –

Patrick isn't the only stranger whose words, spoken in passing, left a weighty impression on my life. Back in 2008, while checking in at the Pittsburgh airport, I overheard a conversation between a customer and a ticket agent that stopped me cold.

The customer was a middle-aged gentleman with a mental disability. When the gate agent asked how he was doing, he responded in the most genuine tone you can imagine, "Wonderfully great," he said with a proud smile.

It was one of those smiles that was pure. I could see it in his eyes; he was thrilled she had inquired about how he was doing.

I couldn't help but smile, too.

When the ticket agent assisted me, we briefly discussed her dialogue with the gentleman. It impacted her profoundly as well. We both agreed that if anyone asked either of us for the rest of the day, we'd both be "wonderfully great."

I have been using that phrase ever since.

# Introduction

I want to look good naked. That's my only goal for living a healthy lifestyle. I don't need to run a seven-minute mile. I don't need my cholesterol level or blood pressure to be within a certain range. I don't need to bench press a baby elephant. I just want to look good with my clothes off. That's been my goal for as long as I can remember. I think I started saying it to get a reaction out of people, especially my mom. But the more I said it, the more it became my truth. My rationale? If I look good naked, that means everything else in my world is probably okay.

Clarification: I don't need to look like an underwear model. I just want to avoid throwing up when I look in the mirror. I don't want to be embarrassed when the sexy nurse at my doctor's office asks me to take off my shirt, and I don't want to have a drawer full of swim shirts.

When I was in college, my metabolism had my back. It never let me down. I lived off Big Macs, Snickers, and soda. I didn't work out. I drank like a fish swimming in a river of whiskey. Did I look good naked? I thought I did. I was skin and bones, but I didn't mind *skinning it* during a pickup basketball game.

I'm not twenty years old anymore.

Now that I'm in my mid- forties, my metabolism has a twisted sense of humor. It taunts me, daring me to go through the drive-thru at McDonald's or pop open a can of Coke. It craves to make me look silly and constantly reminds me I'm getting older. Daily, it screams, "You'd better start doing something different, asshole!"

There are many in the United States who do not hear — or choose to ignore — that deafening call to action. I recently read that by 2030, more than half of Americans will be considered obese. I won't bore you with all the health issues associated with obesity, mainly because you already know what they are: heart disease, diabetes, etc. The problem with our society?

We don't give a shit. We keep eating what we want, and we are chronically sedentary. Then, we bitch and complain we can't fit into those jeans anymore and have to lean on modern medicine to get out of bed and attack life every day.

My biggest fear is to be stuck in the middle of the status quo. Two phrases make me want to run blindfolded through a busy intersection: "You're just like ..." or "you're no different from ..."

I've made a conscious decision to *avoid being* like everyone else, and that is *especially* true when it comes to what I eat and my physical activity. There is just a bigger shock factor when I say, "I want to look good naked."

Spoiler alert: I have taken some radical steps to be the best version of myself. I stopped drinking. I started a running streak of at least 1 mile every day that just turned ten years old. I cut gluten out of my diet. As I'm writing this, I'm also trying out a plant-based diet.

Don't panic!

I'm not going to shove my lifestyle down your throat and won't say you have to start doing *this* or stop doing *that*. I simply want to share what has worked for me. This book is my blueprint. It's my story. It's how I got to the point of enough is enough, stopped making excuses, and started living a bold, adventurous, and intentional life.

And even though these first couple of paragraphs revolve around nutrition and physical activity, this is a complete lifestyle book. It focuses on mental, emotional, and spiritual well-being, and looking good naked.

In other words, this is NOT a diet book. If you feel duped by the title, reach out to me on social media, and I'll make sure you get a full refund. That isn't a joke. If you strictly bought the book based on the title, and you thought you would lose weight by eating tacos and chocolate, I will write you a personal check for the exact amount you spent on this book.

My goals for *Tacos and Chocolate*:

- Give you hope for a better tomorrow
- Inspire you to take action and start living a bold, adventurous, and intentional life

○ Remind you to make the important things important, starting with *you*.

This book targets those who want to take control of their lives, turn the status quo on its head, and put the emphasis on themselves so they can be a light for others. *Tacos and Chocolate* is designed for those running in the quicksand of life and are tired of saying, "I'll do it tomorrow." Whether that's walking away from a hated job, finally climbing Mount Everest, or calling Mom to say, "I love you."

It's important to know this is not a road map or step-by-step guide to a mystical land of rainbows, bubbles, and unicorn farts. I'm not a psychologist or counselor. I'm not a nutritionist or personal trainer. I'm definitely not a priest. I'm not even a self-proclaimed life coach. I'm a regular dude who had eleven jobs in eleven years after graduating from a small state university in Wichita Falls, Texas. I received my degree in journalism, not neuroscience. I do have my master's degree, but it's in educational administration and not behavioral sciences.

Hell, my professional resume includes everything from being a college football coach and real estate agent to working as a radio show host.

I'm just a regular guy.

I'm not rich. I'm not famous. But I do live life on my terms. I'm genuinely happy and have zero regrets. I wake up every morning excited about life. I live with joy, hope, and gratefulness in my heart. I look at everything through the lens of optimism. And I firmly believe love wins. As far as looking good naked goes, I could stand to do more crunches and sit-ups, but it's not too bad. I don't wear the previously mentioned swim shirts at the pool.

This is my story, my journey. This book explains how I got to this point, and what has worked for me.

I want it to inspire *you* to take action. I want you to say these words out loud, "If that guy can do it … I can do it!"

As I shared the concept of this book with several people, a friend of mine lovingly said, "Stop! No one cares. You're different from other people. You have willpower and stick-to-it-ness. People don't want to read that shit!"

She's right. I am different, but I'm not special. I don't have superpowers. I firmly believe that everyone, including you, can make minor lifestyle changes to start living a more satisfying life. Maybe you can take just a few of my suggestions to be the best version of yourself.

About people not wanting to read this book ... I hope she's wrong. Hell, you've already picked it up and read this far.

Let's ride!

But before we jump into my story with both feet, I should probably say that I realize this book is not for everyone.

Regarding physical well-being, maybe you're happy living an unhealthy life. Perhaps you're okay with being overweight. Maybe you're fine with managing your high blood pressure with a little pink pill. If that's the case, put this book down and do you! But you have to do me a favor — you *have* to stop bitching and moaning. You can't do it anymore. You can't eat like shit, not workout, watch enough TV to kill the aforementioned baby elephant, and then constantly complain it's so hard to get out of bed, tie your shoes or play with your kids.

I recently went to dinner with my wife's family. It was her brother, his wife, their grandson, my kids, and my wife's parents. I sat at the end of the table with the kids and let the adults catch up. I was listening, just not engaging. Then they unintentionally baited me. Her brother said, "I don't run, and I don't eat healthy. I hear all the time about people going out for a run and dying from a heart attack or being on a cardboard diet and still getting cancer. I'm going to live life to the fullest, which means no running or working out and eating whatever I want."

I finally spoke up. I couldn't hold my tongue. From the end of the table, I told them, "That is not why people live a healthy lifestyle. If I go out for a run and die, it was my time to go. I run because if I live to be eighty or ninety, I don't want to be bed-ridden or unable to take care of myself. When I'm old, I still want to be living my best life. It's not about avoiding death. It's about really living life."

I got blank stares from the other end of the table. Finally, someone asked, "Can you please pass the fried pickles?"

The problem? My brother-in-law is not the only person in the world who thinks like that. I'm curious, when did eating like crap and being inactive become the definition of living life?

As for mental and emotional wellbeing, maybe you've embraced your pessimistic, glass-half-empty way of thinking. Perhaps you think the phrase, *I'll just do it tomorrow,* is cute and endearing. Maybe you firmly believe you're too *busy* to try something new or make a small change in your life. Again, if that's the case, I'll encourage you to put down this book. Just stop reading. But, just like the people before you who claim to be satisfied with being out of shape, you can't keep grumbling about your job or complain there are not enough hours in the day. You can't keep using the word "busy" like an effing badge of honor; throwing it around as if it validates your existence. You can't stand on the edge of "If Only River" and feel sorry for yourself.

I borrowed that term, the "If Only River" from Max Lucado's *Anxious for Nothing.* Max describes standing on the shore, looking across a body of water at the "Land of the Good Life" and lying to yourself about the reasons you can't have that life by saying things like:

*If only I weighed 15 pounds less...*
*If only the kids were already out of the house...*
*If only I had a little extra money in my bank account...*
*If only I hadn't dropped out of college.*

In other words, you're standing on the bank of that metaphorical river, making excuses for why you can't get to the other side.

With this book, I want to inspire you to take action — to jump headfirst into that raging river and start swimming your ass off. My goal is for you to take just one thing that inspires you to make that leap into the scary water. Not a dozen takeaways. Not five. Not even two. One thing that will positively impact your life and make you stop saying, *If only . . .*

This book is not all about looking good naked in the mirror. I know that's how I began this book, but that was just to grab your attention and make you want to read more. Maybe you already look like Pam Anderson's extra on *Baywatch*, but your emotional and mental wellbeing has been compromised. Perhaps you make a little extra money as an Instagram model, but you're spiritually lost.

I've written *Tacos and Chocolate* to address all aspects of living a healthy life.

One other thing before we officially get going ... there is nothing in this book you haven't heard before. This is not breaking news, but I encourage you to hang with me.

Following one of my speaking gigs, a lady and her husband approached me. She looked me in the eye and said, "You didn't say anything earth-shattering tonight ... I've heard all of that before ... I already knew that stuff." I didn't respond because I knew she had more to say. Then she smirked and continued, "But you were able to take what's spinning around in all of our heads and present it in a way that makes sense. You made it hit home. You made it impactful. Thank you."

That might not have been her exact words. I was still buzzing from Josh Weathers' version of Whitney Houston's "I Will Always Love You." *(Do yourself a favor and Google "Josh Weathers, Whitney." You're welcome.)*

Regardless, her kind words stuck with me. It threw gas on my fire. It made me want to stand in front of more people and share my message. It made me want to write this book.

So, let's ride! *(Spoiler alert: I say that a lot.)*

Oh, why is it called *The Tacos and Chocolate Diet?* You'll find out soon enough!

# 1

## Part I: You Have to Embrace Your Story

*You are the only you God made... God made you and broke the mold.*
*— Max Lucado*

L et's kick off this book with a bet.
  I bet you ten dollars I can make you roll your eyes by simply writing four words.

I'm apprehensive about sharing these four words because some of you will probably put this book down after you read them. Heck, some of you are reading this in the bookstore, and these four words may keep you from purchasing this book. They're going to make you feel *that* uncomfortable.

But I'm going to do it. I have to do it. This needs to be said. It's important.

YOU ARE A MASTERPIECE!

*(Cue the eye-rolling, and you can send my $10 to your favorite non-profit.)*

It's true! You are one-of-a-kind and exquisite. There has never been — and never will be — another person like you.

In the narrative *Memorandum from God*, author Og Mandino writes:

> *Consider a painting by Rembrandt or a bronze by Degas or a violin by Stradivarius or a play by Shakespeare. They have great value for two*

*reasons: their creators were masters and they are few in number. Yet there are more than one of each of these. On that reasoning you are the most valuable treasure on the face of the earth, for you know who cre-ated you and there is only one of you. Never, in all the seventy billion humans who have walked this planet since the beginning of time has there been anyone exactly like you. Never, until the end of time, will there be another such as you.*

Do you know why it makes so many people uncomfortable to read or hear the word *masterpiece*? Because we all know, deep down, we try to avoid and don't like to talk about the fact that it's true. But we've lost sight of that truth.

At the start of *Memorandum from God*, Mandino writes:

*You weep for all your childhood dreams that have vanished with the years.*
*You weep for all your self-esteem that has been corrupted by failure.*
*You weep for all your potential that has been bartered for security.*
*You weep for all your talent that has been wasted through misuse.*
*You look upon yourself with disgrace and you turn in terror from the image you see in the pool. Who is this mockery of humanity staring back at you with bloodless eyes of shame?*

It's hard to consider yourself a masterpiece after life has beaten you down. Mandino writes:

*For how could you be a miracle when you consider yourself a failure at the most menial of tasks? How can you be a miracle when you have lit-tle confidence in dealing with the most trivial of responsibilities? How can you be a miracle when you are shackled by debt ...*

It all comes back to our rarity and our beauty. It comes back to: *Never, in all the seventy billion humans who have walked this planet since the beginning of time has there been anyone exactly like you. Never, until the end of time, will there be another such as you.*

That is why I love the power of story. It celebrates that uniqueness. It highlights that beauty and splendor. Your story is yours and yours alone. My story is mine. No one else can claim our story. No one else can own it. That is why it is so important that we embrace our story — the past, present, and future. The good, the bad, and the ugly.

I've probably said this no less than 1,353 times: I firmly believe we can't live a bold, adventurous, and intentional life until we embrace our story. We have to stop ignoring the parts that suck, the parts that hurt, or the parts that are embarrassing. We have to embrace it all because every aspect of our story has led us right here, to this moment.

Do you want to know my all-time favorite part about the power of story?

It's not over. As long as we're alive, we can rewrite the ending. We have the power to change how our story plays out. We can alter the plot. We can metaphorically kill off characters. We can become heroes. If we're lying face down in the muck, we can pick ourselves up, clean ourselves off, and get back in the fight. If we're already living a wonderfully great life, we can make small changes so we can soar even higher. If we're already standing on top of the mountain, we can reach down and help others reach the summit as well.

Now, I'm not taking the power away from God.

This is my faith talking; He's in control. We can't write an eternal ending for our life. We're not going to live forever. He will ultimately decide the very end. When it's time to go home, God will take us. But I believe, until that moment, he has given us the pen — and the permission — to write a heartfelt and powerful story.

Pushing you to embrace your story is not one of the ultimate goals of this book. I want to give you hope, remind you to make the important things important and inspire you to live boldly, adventurously, and intentionally.

But we can't do those things until we embrace our story. I have zero credibility until I share my story with you — the good, the bad, and the ugly. All of it!

So ... let's start with the ugly.

**Author's Note:** If you don't give two shits about my story, skip to Chapter 17. That's when I share my life lessons and offer practical advice for making small changes in your life. That's the part of the book designed to inspire you and provide that hope I mentioned in the introduction.

In the same breath, if you're still asking yourself, "Who the hell is Drew Myers?!?!?", you probably need to stay the course and move straight into Chapter 2.

# 2

*We can easily forgive a child who is afraid of the dark;*
*the real tragedy of life is when men are afraid of the light.*
*— Plato*

Why does being part of the status quo make me want to take off my boot and throw up into it? Why does the thought of being grouped with everyone else make my anxiety skyrocket? My biggest fear, short of any kind of rodent, is becoming irrelevant and forgotten—leaving this world and having nothing to show for it. I've had this conversation with several people. The overwhelming response has been, "You'll be dead ... it won't matter."

They're right, but that logic doesn't appease me at forty-six years old.

That makes me think of a question I've asked guests on my radio show and podcast many times, "How do you want to be remembered?"

It's important I answer that question. This is me being vulnerable while establishing credibility at the same time.

I want to be remembered as a good dad.

I want to be remembered as a hard worker.

I want to be remembered as witty and funny.

I want to be remembered as kind.

I want to be remembered as someone who brought out the best in other people.

I want to be remembered as witty and funny. *(Oh, did I already say that?)*

As I sat and thought about my legacy *(is that too dramatic?)*, the number one thing that kept popping into my head was that I wanted to be remembered as a person who lived life on his terms.

Recently, I had a guest on my live-audience show use the word "integrity" to describe that *(shout out to the incredible singer/songwriter, Adam Hood)*. After our conversation, I thought about it a lot and put my spin on it. I coined it "self-integrity." My loose definition is "a strong belief and honesty about who I am." Then I did a Google search and realized that was already a thing, and I wasn't the psychology pioneer I thought I was.

One author tied it back to Shakespeare's *Hamlet*. Polonius said, "This above all … to thine own self be true."

Yeah, what that guy said!

I realized that is how I want to be remembered. At my funeral, I want people to say, "He did it his way!"

With that *modus operandi* firmly planted in my subconscious, I constantly strive to be different from everyone else. If most people are zigging, I'm probably going to zag. If they're taking the right fork in the road, I'm probably going to venture down the left side, or skip the fork and go straight to the spoon.

I almost do it defiantly.

"Hold my Topo Chico and gluten-free taco and watch *this!*"

I'm sure if I hadn't stopped going to counseling, that was the next thing my therapist and I were going to discuss. It's the most logical thing to tackle after explaining why I've felt unworthy for most of my adult life *and* revealing I was sexually abused as a child *(both true)*.

Don't worry. I'll give you a heads-up before I share the trauma I endured.

I've never written a book like this before. I've only self-published a little challenge journal back in 2018. I bring that up because I don't know if I can discuss my sexual abuse in the first couple of chapters.

Part of me thinks I'm supposed to save such topics at least until Chapter 8.

But like I said, I've always strayed from doing what I'm supposed to. So here is the heads-up; let's ride. Here are my guts.

- - -

It was a neighbor kid. He was older. Not a lot older, but older. I was only six years old.

This is what I remember: We lived in a redbrick house at the end of a cul-de-sac. A creek ran right behind our house, and was fed by storm tunnels we used to explore. I wrote the F word for the first time on the walls of that tunnel. The house had three bedrooms. My sister's bedroom was at the back of the house — where it happened. We were under the bed for some reason. He made me put his penis in my mouth.

I remember nothing else from the actual encounter. I'm glad I don't.

My next memory, I was sitting on the fireplace hearth in the living room. My parents were sitting across the room on the sofa and the Barcalounger. My older cousin was there. Maybe my grandmother. I assumed it was after the incident in my sister's room, but I later learned that my parents didn't know about that. They sat me down after they found out about another time the neighbor kid preyed on me.

"We don't do that kind of thing." That's what my parents said to me as I sat on the cold stone of the fireplace.

I can't remember if it was my mom or dad who said it, but I recall feeling like it was my fault. I remember feeling like I had done something wrong.

Fast-forward almost thirty-eight years later when all of this resurfaced. I started to have occasional flashes of the incident. They would pop into my mind at the most random times. It was like watching a drive-in movie in the fog.

Here's an example.

I was the sports director at a summer camp for neglected and abused children. I was the fun guy who got to coordinate water balloon fights and dodgeball tournaments. It was awesome. The kids were great — full of life.

After the week-long camp, there was a debriefing with all the counselors. That's when they told us about the kids, specifically their troubled backgrounds. It was my first year working at the camp. Most of the other counselors already knew the kids' stories. I didn't. I knew they came from broken homes and terrible situations, but I was unprepared for the information they shared in that wrap-up meeting.

They told the counselors every kid at the camp had experienced abuse in some capacity. Ninety-five percent of the kids there had been abused by someone in their life. My heart broke. I could not get their faces and beautiful smiles out of my head.

That number — ninety-five percent — stuck with me for a couple of weeks. Then those personal flashes started happening.

Under my sister's bed.

Neighbor kid.

Fireplace hearth.

"We don't do that kind of thing."

Then, I asked myself questions about the camp.

"Should I have been there?"

"What if they found out I was also sexually abused?"

"Should I have told them?"

"Could I get in trouble?"

"Did I do something wrong … again?"

I said nothing to anyone until I went on a sibling trip to New Orleans that same summer. It was my two younger sisters, Susan and Allison, me, and our spouses. It was a quick getaway from our kiddos.

There was a lot of yummy food and booze. That's when I was firmly off the wagon. (*I was actually driving it that weekend. On that trip, I tried to drink all the Jameson and ginger ale in the Big Easy.*)

On our last night there, we were at a nice dinner, and I told my sisters about the abuse. I don't know why the abuse came up, but it did. Maybe it was the Jameson. Perhaps I needed to talk about it.

My sisters had no clue. I spoke freely about what happened, reiterating it wasn't the actual abuse I was wrestling with; it was my parents' response to the abuse. My mind constantly went back to that fireplace hearth.

When we got home from New Orleans, my mom texted me immediately. My middle sister, Susan, thought our mom should know about our "light" dinner conversation. Mom asked if I was okay. I assured her I was, but she still wanted to sit down and talk.

My mom, dad, wife, and kids went to dinner a couple of days later. We talked through it. Again, I reassured her I was fine.

At that point, following the all-in-the family "are you okay" dinner, I thought, and hoped, those skeletons were officially locked away forever.

Then, my heart told me to share this experience on my radio show and podcast. It wasn't planned. I didn't have it in my show notes. It just happened.

I had met with a spiritual mentor that morning, and the abuse came up — specifically my head trash surrounding my self-worth. I told her I didn't feel worthy of love or God's blessings.

I mentioned that realization and hard truth to my co-host later in the day, and she lovingly pushed. She wanted me to share — on the air. I took a deep breath and, for the first time ever, talked openly about my sexual abuse as a child. It was freeing. I felt like I could finally breathe. But then reality punched me in the testicles, and every ounce of air left my body. I realized the segment we had just recorded was going to run in the next forty-eight hours. The world was about to hear my darkest secret. And by "world," I mean the couple of hundred people who actually listened to the show regularly at that point. That did not ease my anxiety.

We released the podcast episode in the afternoon. My mom stopped by my house that morning before it ran.

"I heard I need to listen to your podcast," she said as we stood around my kitchen island.

"It's pretty heavy," I said.

"Are you okay?"

I'm not sure why she kept asking me that, but she did.

"I'm good. It was on my heart to share . . . so, I did."

We talked through some things that morning. For example, that's when I found out I was six years old when it happened. We talked about the abuse itself, too – specifically the incident under my sister's bed. My mom told me she didn't even know about that particular time. She said she only knew about the time two neighbor boys chained me to our swing set and molested me, an incident I have no memory of.

I'm grateful I don't remember any of that.

My mom told me she and my dad were out furniture shopping when they got a call. This was before cell phones, so my cousin had to figure out where they were and call the store.

I learned the confrontation on the fireplace hearth happened after they had gotten home from furniture shopping. After I was chained to a swing set.

My parents' response to the abuse is what haunts me. Thinking back to that moment is what makes me push to be different. To be seen and relevant. To be remembered. All these years later, I hear my parents' words, "We don't do things like that."

In my mind, I wasn't special enough to be protected. I didn't deserve to be safe from predatory assholes who lived on my cul-de-sac. At that moment, I didn't feel cared for or loved; I felt shame.

As an adult, I vowed to do everything in my power to be special in my weird and twisted subconscious, to do things differently. To not fall into the status quo.

I didn't want to be that six-year-old boy sitting on that fireplace hearth ever again.

After my mom listened to the show, she sent me a text.

Mom: *I listened to your podcast. I didn't cry, but I feel indescribably sad that you somehow felt we weren't taking care of you or loving you enough. No doubt we didn't handle it correctly. Based on what you told me this morning, there must have been more than one incident, and we were too stupid to know. I'm so sorry. P.S. I pray for you. Ily.*

I told her via text it was in the past, and it didn't define me.

Me: *I don't hold anything against you guys. You did the best you could.*

Mom: *Well, we should have done better.*

I simply wrote back, *I love you.*

Mom: *I hope you know how much I love you.*

Me: *I do, Mom. Promise.*

# 3

*Parenthood . . . it's about guiding the next generation
and forgiving the last.*
*— Peter Krause*

I have daddy issues. There, I said it.

I think some of it must have to do with sitting on that fireplace hearth after my neighbor made me do things a six-year-old should never be forced to do. In my subconscious, I hear those words echoing, — "We don't do things like that."

Do you want to know the funny part of that story? I think it was my mom who said those words, not my dad.

But in my mind, it was my dad who was supposed to protect me. All these years later, that is the narrative I've been telling myself. Don't forget, this all happens in my subconscious. I don't think about this all the time. I don't dwell on it. I refuse to give that asshole neighbor that much power.

But that story — and my overall relationship with my father — has played a significant role in my life.

My dad wasn't a bad dad. He was always around. We didn't necessarily do the stereotypical father-son things (*play catch, go fishing, build shit, etc.*), but he was present. I knew he loved me, but he didn't say those words very often. I knew he was proud of me but only because his friends would talk about him bragging about me.

I'm putting all these disclaimers in this chapter because I know there are people out there whose parents were much worse than mine. They were horrible. They were absent. They were abusive. They didn't care.

That wasn't my dad. The worst thing he ever did was say, "The bad part about having kids — they're always around." We've all thought that, right? He just said it out loud.

My biggest issues with my father were lack of communication and lack of affection. That hurt me growing up. If he hadn't showered my sisters with love and admiration, I would not have known the difference. But he did, and I didn't understand why. The best adjective to describe my dad's parenting philosophy toward me would probably be tough love.

As I began writing this chapter, I looked for an example of that toughness. I was going through an old keepsake box, and I stumbled across a letter my dad wrote to me in my senior year of college. I don't remember receiving the letter. I may have blocked it out, since it said some disheartening things.

Here are some excerpts:

*Mom said you were upset about me trying to tell you what to do with your life ... maybe you will understand where I am coming from when you have children of your own. You are going to want the best for them and will do just about anything to see them do their best.*

*I never wanted to interfere in your decisions, or for you to feel obligated to please me by doing anything that you didn't want to do.*

*I will continue to watch for the perfect job for you, I will just keep it to myself. Deal?*

*Drew, I really do love you, and I want you to do your very best, at whatever you choose. Keep this letter, it may be the only one you ever get from me, and read it when you want to tell your son what he should do with his life.*

When I found that letter, it made my heart heavy and my eyes filled with tears.

This chapter is a response to that letter. As I continue to tell my story, this will hopefully help you understand why I do what I do — my motives and driving force.

This is an open letter I wrote to my father (*I wrote this as part of a homemade Christmas gift in 2001*):

*Dear Dad,*

*I'm so sorry it took me so long to respond, but I guess later is better than never. The purpose of this letter is to tell you that I'M sorry. I don't think this is a newsflash for either one of us, but you know that we haven't had the best communication skills in our relationship. Remember when I was in high school, and we went round and round about some of the stupidest things. We were both stubborn. We banged heads about anything and everything. There were a few occasions where I honestly thought one of us was going to take a swing. I'm sorry.*

*After I left for college, our relationship got a lot better. (But based on this letter, obviously it wasn't great.)*

*But I would consider our relationship great today.*

*I just wanted to say that I'm sorry for all that wasted time. Looking back, I was to blame for 90 percent of our problems. You didn't have to write me a letter and tell me that you were just looking out for my best interest. I knew you were. I think I got "upset," because I just wanted to make you proud. That's all I've ever wanted to do.*

*Remember that fight we had after I missed a football practice my sophomore year of high school? You have no idea how mad I was at myself — simply because I let you down. The fact you wanted me to take a drug test didn't exactly make me happy, but I was still more upset at myself — not you. I'm sorry.*

*When we got into it about Paul (a gay friend of mine in high school), I thought that I was letting you down because I was hanging out with someone who was homosexual. Stupid. I know. I am sorry something as trivial as the sexual preference of one of my friends caused ripples in our relationship.*

*Don't worry, I never felt "obligated to please you" by doing something that I didn't want to do, but I'll tell you right now ... you've played a role in every decision that I've ever made.*

*Over the years, I've constantly asked myself: "Would this make my dad proud?"*

*That has always been a staple of my decision-making process. If the answer was no, you can bet your ass that I wasn't going to do it.*

*Dad, I know that you're proud of me. You've never said it to me in so many words, but I know you are. You have no idea how wonderfully great it makes me feel when one of your friends says: "I've heard all about you. Your dad is so proud."*

*Dad, I hope I continue to make you proud, in whatever I do. I love you and once again ... I'm sorry.*

*Drew*

I told you ... daddy issues.

One thing I didn't mention in the letter ... my perfect attendance streak. From the first grade until I graduated from high school, I missed only one day of school. That one absence was my senior year.

Starting in the first grade, I went to school every day no matter what.

When I share that fun fact, people look at me in shock and awe. Going to school every day was an easy decision because it was important to my dad. He loved telling people about my perfect attendance. I could tell he was proud of me. I didn't want to let him down.

The only day of school I missed in those twelve years was after hand surgery. I tore the tendon in my right ring finger playing football. My surgery was scheduled on a school day, and my dad was disappointed.

I remember waking up in the recovery room, throwing up all over myself — compliments of the anesthesia — and my dad saying, "If we get you up right now, we can still get you to school in time so they don't count you absent."

He may have been kidding, but it still upset me that I had let him down. I laid in that hospital bed beating myself up.

My hand looked like Dr. Frankenstein had been brought in for the procedure, and the room smelled like throw-up, but all I could think about was disappointing my dad. I remember lying there, wishing nausea away so I could get up and go to school. All I wanted to do was make him proud.

– – –

I didn't know my dad's father. Edgar Myers passed away before I was born. I've been told that everyone called him Ed. In my mind, he was the stereotypical, early century, non-emotion-expressing, tough dad. There have been moments in my life when I hated that man, which isn't fair at all. I hated him because my father inherited many of those character traits from him and brought them into our relationship.

When I was writing this book, I thought it was important to learn more about my grandfather. This was hard for me to do, though.

Sidebar: Every day, one of the things I write on my to-do list is, "Do one thing that scares me."

Well, having this conversation with my dad about his father scared me. Why? I think a lot of it had to do with my dad and I didn't communicate like that. A normal conversation between my dad and me was usually short, sweet, and to the point. Heart-to-heart talks had never been our thing. We avoided intimacy.

I treaded lightly when we would get into a conversation that was more than surface level. I never wanted to say the wrong thing and upset him. That had happened many times throughout my life. He had an amazing gift of taking what I said and twisting it into a personal knot of self-deprecation. The letter he sent me while I was in college is a perfect example of that. If I didn't embrace or agree with his idea, no matter how big or small, he would get his feelings hurt. I could see it in his eyes. He thought I didn't appreciate his ideas, thoughts, or feedback. He felt stupid.

Regarding the conversation about his father, I was anxious because I didn't want my dad to read into my questions. I didn't want him to think I was trying to psychoanalyze our relationship. I didn't want him to wonder about my motives for having the conversation. I also didn't want him to think that I thought he was a bad dad.

Acknowledging those thoughts was enlightening. It made me realize I was probably the source of many of the communication issues over the years.

Anyway, I wanted and needed to have this conversation with my dad about my grandfather. Let's ride!

We were on a family getaway at Christmas. It was my wife and kids, my folks, and my sisters' families. All the grandkids were there. I woke up early to write, and I was working on this chapter about my daddy issues. When the house came alive, I made a conscious decision to ask my dad about Ed.

As we drank coffee that morning, my dad shared some one-off stories about his father. He talked about when he died. My dad was twenty-three. My mom also told stories about him she had heard over the years. My dad even called his sister to see if she had a story or two to contribute.

My grandfather was a quiet man who suffered from depression. That was my biggest takeaway from our conversation that morning. He would go days without saying a word and then unload his over-analyzed head trash.

I think that stuck with me because those were two traits my dad inherited, and they played a huge role in our relationship — as I was growing up and even into adulthood.

Our conversation that morning just reinforced what I already knew. I wasn't surprised by the picture they painted of my grandfather.

That is why I was mad at him — a man I had never known — for a long time. I projected that anger onto my father. In hindsight, that bitterness was the primary source of a lot of our issues — especially regarding communication. It took me more than forty years and dozens of therapy sessions to unpack that.

I remember the moment I let that anger go, my relationship with my father changed.

We were living under my parents' roof when it happened. When I say "we," I mean myself, my wife, and my two children. I was forty years old. We had moved from Fort Worth to Rainbow, Texas, to build a house on my family's property, which was on the banks of the Brazos River. I won't bore you with why it took two years to get our house built, but we lived with my mom and dad the entire time. It wasn't a terrible experience, but here is some unsolicited advice: Adult children, and their families, should avoid living with their folks at all costs — especially for two years.

Anyway, during this transition in my life, I went out for a run one night. I had a short route around their house that I did regularly, especially after the sun went down. It was about a quarter-mile, and I would do it at least four times to keep my daily running streak alive. I was a city boy, still getting used to running in the country. At night, I didn't like to get too far from the house. I'm not a fan of nocturnal critters.

During this particular run, I stopped and prayed. I was outside the glow of the floodlights on the corner of the house. The stars were bright, which is common in Rainbow, Texas. They seemed brighter that night, though.

I told God I wanted to forgive my dad. I told Him I didn't want to hold on to that hurt and anger anymore. I said I understood why my father loved the way he loved. I added that I knew enough about my grandfather to show my father grace.

*Lord, my dad did the best he could. I know he loves me. He always has.*

*I recognize his father didn't express his love, like my dad surely needed growing up. Everyone needs that, God! My dad was simply playing with the cards he was dealt — what he knew. He loved the way his dad loved him. For a long time, I was mad about that. The anger was real because I didn't understand. I choose to forgive my dad. I give all the anger and hurt to you, God. Help me heal. Help us heal. Amen.*

I took a deep breath — deeper than normal — and it felt like one of the donkeys on our property had jumped off my shoulders. I looked up at the stars. They seemed even brighter than before. I smiled.

As I started to run again, a wave of peace engulfed me, and I whispered, "Thank you."

# 4

*Some people drift through their entire life.*
*They do it one day at a time, one week at a time, one month at a time.*
*It happens so gradually they are unaware*
*of how their lives are slipping away until it's too late.*
*– Mary Kay Ash*

**M**any times, when I'm speaking to a group, I'll share a fun fact that seems to make everyone in the room a little uncomfortable. I address this during my speech or presentation by saying:

> *I'm about to tell you guys something about myself that will either make you judge me or feel sorry for me. There are some people in this room that are going to start feeling a little uneasy. Some of you are going to shift a little in your chairs, but some of you are going to think to yourselves, 'I should have gone to the other break-out session.'*

When I mentioned the following fun fact in the intro of this book, I was serious.

After I graduated from Midwestern State University in Wichita Falls, Texas, I had eleven jobs in eleven years. While my dad had trouble expressing his love and affection, he was never short on advice. Some of it was excellent advice. He told me growing up, "If you're not happy with what you're doing ... go do something else."

Well, I embraced that philosophy with both arms and squeezed tight.

My dad used to share this story about his friend, Bill Shaw. Bill worked for Mary Kay cosmetics. I've probably heard my dad tell this story no less than sixty-three times.

This is my spin on it:

> One morning, Bill woke up to his alarm clock going off. He rolled out of bed and began his morning routine. He walked into the bathroom and brushed his teeth. As he stared at himself in the mirror — through the sleep in his eyes — he thought, I actually heard my alarm clock go off this morning. That's weird.
>
> He shrugged it off and continued to get ready for work.
>
> While pouring his cereal later that morning, he had the same thought, "My alarm clock woke me up this morning. So weird. That never happens."
>
> On his way to work, he thought the same thing again. When he got to the office, he walked straight into his boss's office and shared the story of hearing his alarm clock go off. His boss told him he needed to find another job.
>
> Bill, who might have been a big deal with Mary Kay, wasn't getting fired, but his boss (shout out to Mary Kay Ash) recognized Bill had lost his fire for the iconic company. His boss must've realized Bill wasn't excited to jump out of bed and come to work. Bill's boss helped him realize that.

I have no idea if this story is true. My dad tended to fabricate tall tales, but it's irrelevant. I understood — even from a young age — the symbolism behind the story of Bill Shaw and his alarm clock. If you love what you do, you're passionate about it, you should be excited to jump out of bed and attack the day. Screw the alarm clock. I do know Bill left

Mary Kay and went to start his own successful company. That gave the story some validity.

I'm passionate about what I do now. I love it. It fires me up. But I hear my alarm clock go off every morning. I hear it go off two or three times because I'm addicted to the snooze button.

Now, back to those eleven jobs in eleven years. I'll give you a brief timeline before I was introduced to the power of autosuggestion and how that catapulted me to First Class. *(In radio, that is called a tease.)*

Right out of college, I worked in the newspaper industry. Since that's what my folks and I spent thousands of dollars to study in college, I thought that's what I was supposed to do after I graduated. I finished school at MSU with a degree in mass communications and a minor in journalism. My first real job was on the copy desk at *The Times Record News*, the newspaper in Wichita Falls. It was a safe first job since I worked on the sports desk while I was going to school. I remember when I interviewed for the job on the other side of the newsroom.

The Managing Editor asked, "What do you want to be when you grow up?"

"A roadie in a band!" I answered.

In any other job interview — with someone that didn't already know me — my smart-ass answer probably would have cost me the job. But they were already familiar with me, my work ethic, and my personality. They offered me the position. I accepted, and I stayed exactly one year.

That's when I decided I needed to spread my wings and fly. I had outgrown Wichita Falls, and I wanted to see another part of the country. I applied to newspapers across the United States. I ended up a feature designer for the *Medford Mail Tribune* in Southern Oregon. I told you part of the story in the book's preface. Don't forget, I moved up there with a college buddy *(shout out to Chris Gilliand, again)* where we met a homeless man who dropped this nugget of inspiration on me, "I don't want things to happen accidentally. I want things to happen on purpose."

I had an amazing experience, but I was only there for one year because I missed my mommy.

Now, I know this is supposed to be a snapshot of my eleven jobs in eleven years after graduating from college, but I have to share a couple of highlights from my 365 days in Oregon. It was exactly one year from the time I pulled into town to the day I headed back to Texas.

Highlights from my adventure on the left coast:

- Chris and I were homeless for the first three weeks we were there. We lived in tents at a campsite outside of town. I would go to work at the newspaper during the day while Chris tried to find us a place to live. Our stuff was in a storage unit in Ashland, Oregon. We entertained ourselves by making up games while throwing rocks in the river.
- I fell in love with nature and the outdoors during that year. We hiked. We snow skied. We fished. We smoked weed.
- I quickly learned how much I loved Texas and how proud I was to be from the Lone Star State.
- I realized I didn't want to be in the newspaper industry for the rest of my life.

When I moved to Oregon, I never dreamed I'd be there for only one year. But it was time to go home. Over those 365 days, I became very aware of how much I loved my family. I truly did miss them. Not to mention, I was terrified my dad would have another heart attack, and I wouldn't be able to get home fast enough. All flights out of the small Medford airport went to Portland or San Francisco before Dallas. Traveling out of Southern Oregon was tough and not conducive to a father with congestive heart failure.

I moved to Oregon in a twenty-foot U-Haul truck. I moved back to Texas with whatever fit in the back of my Jeep Grand Cherokee. I sold the rest or gave it to Chris.

I remember driving over Siskiyou Pass into California with tears streaming down my face. I was listening to *Fire and Rain* on repeat *(shout out to James Taylor)*. Why was I crying like an idiot? There were several reasons. I felt like I was abandoning Chris. I felt as if I had failed on my adventure to the Pacific Northwest. And even though I had a job waiting for me back home, a wave of uncertainty overwhelmed me.

But I think the main reason I got so emotional was because it was a safe and impregnable decision at that point in my life. I wasn't just driving back to Texas. I was going back to a place of familiarity and comfort. As bold as it was to pack up and move to Oregon, this was on the other end of the spectrum. I was heading back to a place I knew well. I think the best adjective I can use to describe the decision to move home is "safe."

Some people love that feeling. It made me cry like an idiot.

I had already accepted a job at my alma mater as an admissions counselor at Midwestern State. That was the only adventurous part of this decision, and what ultimately gave me peace. I was getting out of the newspaper industry. It was significant because a small part of me still thought it to be my predetermined fate — for no other reason than the naïve fact I got my degree in journalism.

I wasn't just changing jobs. I was changing professions. And all the whispers — from Bill Shaw to Crazy Joe — finally made the tears stop.

As I made my first rest stop in Weed, California, I became excited about the next chapter of my life.

# 5

*Unless a man believes in himself and makes a total commitment*
*to his career and puts everything he has into it — his mind, his body, his*
*heart — what's life worth to him?*
*– Vince Lombardi*

I'm going to fast-forward through a few years. They are part of my story, but I'm excited to share how the power of autosuggestion impacted my life. Autosuggestion is when your subconscious mind takes over and helps your dreams become reality.

After leaving Oregon and taking the job at Midwestern State in Wichita Falls, I settled into Texas living. I also got used to working outside the newspaper industry. I was kind of digging this brand-new world. As an admissions counselor at a state university, I started the work day at 8 a.m., went to lunch from noon to 1 p.m., and left work at 5 o'clock. Every day. Like clockwork. I didn't get to work at 7:59 a.m. or stay until 5:01 p.m. I worked 8 hours a day — not a second more.

I had no idea what to do with myself. I had more time on my hands than I had ever had. Unlike when I worked at a newspaper, my nights were now free. And I was also back in the town where I went to college. So, how I filled my newfound free time will not be a huge shock to anyone ... I drank like I owned stock in Jack Daniel's Whiskey. I was a mess. I wouldn't even go home after work. I'd go straight to the bar. If I didn't have a beer or cocktail in front of me by 5:10 p.m., something was terribly wrong. I usually stumbled home around midnight and slept a few hours so I could do it all again the next day.

Then, I started traveling for my job. I traveled across the state to recruit high school seniors to attend Midwestern. I lived out of hotel rooms four to five days a week *(shout out to La Quinta)*. This went on for weeks and weeks at a time. When I worked out of the office in Wichita Falls, I partied hard. When I was on the road, I partied like I was Eddie Van Halen. My liver was pissed off, and as much as I thought I was living my best life ... I was not!

During this rock star season of my life, I went to a random wedding with my sister, Susan, in Houston. She needed a date and easily coaxed me with the guarantee of there being an open bar. Did I mention I was a drunken mess?

At this random wedding for one of Susan's sorority sisters — who I only knew vaguely — I met a girl *(shout out to Amy Holmes)*. I use the term "met" pretty loosely. I talked to her for two minutes that night in a dark parking lot.

I saw her during the reception and watched her from across the room all night. *(It's only weird if you make it weird.)* She was with her parents and grandparents, who were all family friends of the bride's parents. When they were leaving, I chased her down in the dark parking lot I just mentioned. I told her I couldn't let her leave without telling her I thought she was beautiful. I was drunk. Her entire family was standing there when I told her I had watched her from across the room all night. It was awkward. I had officially made it weird.

But I ended up falling in love with this girl.

After the random wedding and my parking lot confession, I went back to Wichita Falls. This mystery girl lived in Houston, which was almost six hours away. I guess she must have admired my boldness or ability to hold my liquor, because she found me online, remembering I had mentioned working at MSU.

When I got to work on Monday morning, I had an email from Amy waiting for me. We traded emails regularly after that. After a few months of emailing, we eventually met up again. Then, we were intentional about seeing each other regularly – 375 miles be damned.

I had fallen head over heels for her.

One of the main reasons I fell in love with her was because she made me want to be a better person. She made me want to turn down the knob on drinking, and start working out. From six hours away, she made me want to be the best version of myself. To this day, I'm grateful to her for helping me get my life back on track.

Amy also inadvertently helped me realize it was time to change professions *again*.

Here's the timeline: That random wedding was in the spring of 2000. The next fall, after Amy and I turned up the knob on our long-distance relationship and I was getting my shit together, I asked the million-dollar question, "What the hell am I doing with my life?"

I remember this vividly. I was doing a college fair in Seagoville, Texas. I stood behind my table, clad in its maroon MSU table drape. I'm sure I was wearing khakis and an oversized sports coat that I had bought off the rack. The event was in the Seagoville High School gym with all the other college recruiters. That musty gym smell was ever present. None of the students at the school gave two shits that I was there. They didn't want to discuss going to school at Midwestern State University. They wanted to talk to the recruiters from Texas A&M, LSU, and Oklahoma State. I just stood there and smiled like an idiot.

I remember looking around the gym, tucking my lips, and shaking my head. That's when I asked myself that monumental question. "What the hell am I doing with my life?"

I knew it was time for a change. I knew I wanted to be closer to Amy. I knew I wanted to find my true calling.

I wanted to coach college football.

Yep! This former long-haired, narcissistic journalism major — who had a bachelor's degree in mass communications — decided he wanted to be a football coach.

It's the logical step, right?

Here was the unimpressive resume I was bringing to the table: I graduated with that degree in mass comm. I had already burned through three jobs in the four years after receiving my diploma. None of them in college athletics, and none of them involving a ball. I had played high school football. I had played intramural football in college, too. The biggest feather in my cap, I had recently read Vince Lombardi's biography, *When Pride Still Mattered*.

Here was my illustrious game plan:

○ Quit my salaried job at MSU;
○ Move to the Greater Houston area to be closer to my girlfriend, who I had been dating for less than a year;
○ Wait tables for the first six months;
○ Walk-on and play football at Blinn College, which was about 70 miles outside of Houston, then
○ Be a coach.

Yes, I was going to play college football at twenty-seven years old. Stop giggling. I thought that's what I had to do to chase my new dream of coaching college football and being the next Vince Lombardi. I had done my research, and almost every head coach on the collegiate level had played college football.

The next step was securing a spot on the roster.

So, I sent emails to the head coach at Blinn. No response.

I sent a letter. Crickets.

Every time I called, no one answered the phone.

I was deterred, but I refused to fold. Don't forget, I was waiting tables at Texas Land and Cattle with a bachelor's degree during all of this. Even though I was the Employee of the Month on two occasions at the restaurant, I had bigger aspirations. So, I eventually drove an hour from my new apartment on the west side of Houston and knocked on the door of the Blinn Football Office. One of the coaches was sitting at the front desk *(shout out to Brad Beerwinkel)*. He didn't even get up to answer the door. He just yelled for me to come in.

I introduced myself, asked if they were having trouble with their phones, and I told him about my game plan. He laughed. Not at my attempted humor about the antiquated phone system, but about my dreams of playing college football.

I guess he saw the disappointment in my eyes after his yuk because it was there.

He tried to soften the blow, explaining why I couldn't play football at Blinn. He cited NCAA and junior college eligibility rules. He also said I would get my head bashed in. But he did say they could always use a volunteer coach on the staff.

"You mean I can coach college football without playing college football?" I asked.

"Yep!" he said.

"That is awesome, but just for the record ... I wouldn't get my head bashed in."

Laughing uncontrollably, he said, "Okay."

"I'm so excited!"

"You *do* understand that we're not going to be able to pay you, right?"

I told him I didn't care. My dream was alive, *and* I got to skip one step in my preconceived plan of attack.

I scheduled a meeting with the head football coach to discuss being a volunteer coach.

On my drive back to Houston, I thought, *This is really going to happen.*

– – –

When I started volunteering in the football office at Blinn, they immediately gave me a very important title, "Coach." I didn't have to sign a piece of paper, making it official. I didn't have to fill out a registration form or apply for a special card to carry in my wallet.

In a blink, I was "Coach Myers."

The first time one of the Blinn football players called me Coach Myers, a wave of emotion hit me. We were in the weight room, and my new journey had officially begun. That wave of emotion was highlighted by the risk I had taken to end up in that weight room.

After meeting with the head football coach (*shout out to Everett Todd*), I was hired as the defensive backs coach at Blinn College. It was an unpaid position, but they gave me a meal card for the cafeteria and a couch to sleep on in the field house if I didn't feel like driving back to Houston after a long night at the football office.

I loved every aspect of my new role — from being on the field to helping with operations off the field, including academics and recruiting. My favorite part was engaging and mentoring the players.

Even though I felt like an impostor with a whistle for a while, every time someone referred to me as "Coach," it made me smile the biggest smile. That title was a constant reminder of the wild and crazy ride I took to accomplish that dream. I loved it.

As time passed, I felt less and less like a poser because I grew in my new profession. I realized there was so much more that went along with that title. The responsibility. The organization. The student-athletes. The passion. The caring. The game.

I loved all of that more than the title itself.

I remember driving back to my apartment in Houston late one night after a two-a-day practice before the season started. I passed an industrial complex where guys were busting their asses in the glow from the factory and the lights from the heavy machinery.

*I am so fortunate*, I thought. *I was intentional about chasing my dream, and now I'm living it.*

I was grateful for the opportunity I had at Blinn. I was thankful I didn't have to work the night shift at a Houston industrial plant. I couldn't stop wondering if those guys working at that factory had big dreams, too. Were they living those dreams? Were they happy? Had their dreams died? Why did they die? How did they die? Was there still time for them to change their life and chase those dreams?

I refocused on my situation, counting my blessings for this incredible opportunity at Blinn. As I continued driving down 290 toward Houston, a wave of peace engulfed me, and I whispered, "Thank you."

– – –

Over the next two and a half years working at Blinn, I survived a coaching change, became a dorm mommy, broke up with the girl I legitimately thought I would marry, got my Master's degree, and met my wife at a family reunion.

I guess I wouldn't be doing my job as the author of this book if I didn't briefly touch on each of those life events:

– *About the coaching change:* After my first year on Coach Todd's staff, they fired him. I told the new coach *(shout out to Scott Maxfield)* I was dedicated to Blinn Football, not necessarily to the previous coach. I asked Coach Maxfield for the opportunity to stay on the staff. I think it helped that I wasn't getting paid, but he gave me a chance. He moved me to the defensive side of the ball and put me in charge of recruiting.

– *About being a "dorm mommy":* As part of the agreement to keep me on the football staff, I had to move into one of the Blinn dorms and make sure the 80-something guys who lived there didn't burn the place down. I had a small apartment on the first floor. I lived there rent-free. I got to eat in the cafeteria for free. It wasn't a horrible setup. I only had a handful of incidents with the eighty-something guys under my care. The biggest escapade was when someone purposely tried to flood the first floor of the building. They clogged all the drains in the bathroom, turned on the showers and the sink faucets, locked the bathroom door from the inside, and crawled out the bathroom window. This resulted in a big mess and me being woken up at 3:30 in the morning.

– *About the break up:* There really isn't much to say about this. I saw a legitimate future for us. She didn't. We split up. In hindsight, I think her parents hated the fact she was dating a football coach and dorm mommy. I think that because that's what they told her. It just wasn't meant to be.

– *About graduate school:* In August 2004, I graduated from Prairie View A&M with my master's degree in educational administration. A lot of coaches had encouraged me to get a master's in something, so I did. I've never used that degree in any of my jobs, and I actually had to dig through boxes in my attic to find my diploma so I could reference it in this book. I needed to remind myself exactly when I graduated.

– *About meeting my wife at a family reunion:* On a football recruiting trip to Austin, my "cousin" Kriste invited me to swing by her mom's house and go out with her and others. I refer to Kriste as my "cousin" because she's not my cousin. We're not related by blood in any shape, form, or fashion. Her mom and my uncle have been dating since Kriste and I were kids. I guess that's as close as you can get to being related while staying off each other's family tree. Kriste wanted me to come over that night, so I could meet her actual cousin, Tanya. Even though I grew up with Kriste, I didn't know Tanya existed. After we went out that night, we started talking. We fell in love, and we got married in the summer of 2004.

My next professional adventure began the day after we got back from our honeymoon.

# 6

*I don't want things to happen accidentally.*
*I want things to happen on purpose.*
*— Patrick (a.k.a. Crazy Joe)*

The power of autosuggestion played a huge role in the next chapter of my life.

After starting out as a volunteer coach at Blinn College and forced to learn the ins and outs of coaching on the fly, I was eventually elevated to full-time status. After each season, I received a promotion going from a volunteer coach to an unpaid graduate assistant and eventually to a full-time coach. (They also gave me the opportunity to relinquish my duties as a dorm mom.)

From the time I left Wichita Falls — and my full-time job in the admissions office — it was a mind-blowing whirlwind of events.

But after three seasons of coaching at the junior college level, I wanted more. Just like all of our players at Blinn, I had dreams of going Division I. They wanted to play football at schools like the University of Texas, LSU, and Oklahoma, and I wanted to coach at the same types of schools. Division I football is the biggest stage for college sports.

The bad news was I wasn't exactly sure how I was going to accomplish that goal.

The good news was my subconscious was already working overtime to make that dream a reality.

This is when I accidentally fell in love with the psychological technique of autosuggestion, which was developed by Émile Coué in the early twentieth century. He wrote: "... autosuggestion is an instrument that we possess at birth, and in this instrument, or rather in this force, resides a marvelous and incalculable power, which according to circumstances produces the best or the worst results."

In the wonderfully great book *Think and Grow Rich*, Napoleon Hill breaks it down to its simplest form, "Autosuggestion is the power to influence your subconscious mind."

Let me whittle it down even more. Napoleon Hill had a step-by-step guide to accomplish this goal:

Step 1: Figure out what you want.
Step 2: Focus on it.
Step 3: Say out loud that you will get it.
Step 4: Believe in your heart you will get it.
Step 5: Repeat Steps 2-4

Expanding on Mr. Hill's explanation, you're influencing your subconscious mind to get exactly what you want.

One of the most famous autosuggestion stories is about actor Jim Carey writing himself a $10 million check when he was a struggling comedian in Hollywood. He said he wrote the check to make himself feel better. He postdated it ten years and put it in his wallet. It was for "acting services rendered," and Carey's mind trick worked. In 1996, he was paid $15 million for the sequel to *Ace Ventura: Pet Detective*.

As a junior college football coach in central Texas, it wasn't about what I wanted; it was about where I wanted to go.

I wanted to coach at Texas Christian University, an up-and-coming powerhouse in college football. More importantly, TCU was the hometown team in Dallas/Fort Worth. That's where I grew up and where my immediate family lives. I wanted to go home and coach for the Horned Frogs. *Step 1 – Figure out what you want: Check!*

I quickly raced through Steps 2-4 without even knowing what I was doing.

One of our players at Blinn, who was being recruited by TCU, received a postcard in the mail from one of the Horned Frog coaches. On the postcard was a picture of TCU's Amon G. Carter Stadium at dusk. There were no players on the field and no fans in the bleachers, but the lights brightly shined on this college football temple.

After reading the postcard, our player threw it away. Receiving a postcard wasn't anything special. They received a lot of mail from a lot of different schools; it happened all the time. However, this time, I picked it out of the trash and hung the photo on my bulletin board in the football office. I whispered to myself, "That's where I want to go."

Every time I sat at my desk, I would look at that postcard. My dream of coaching at TCU was in my face every day. *Step 2 – Focus on it: Check!*

Later that season, I was introduced to the TCU football program firsthand. We were on our way to play a road game in Oklahoma, and we had arranged to practice at the Horned Frogs' facilities along the way. This gave me my first glimpse inside a Division I football program. When I stepped back onto the team bus after our walk-thru, I told the rest of the Blinn coaching staff, "This is where I'm going, and I'm never coming back." *Step 3 – Say out loud you will get it: Check!*

It was a brash and bold statement, but I was dead serious. Deep down in my soul, I believed that's where I was going. *Step 4 – Believe in your heart you will get it: Check!*

During the spring of 2004, I received a call from TCU's Director of Football Operations, Mike Sinquefield. His assistant position had come open, and he remembered me expressing interest at one point. This is important to know: While my subconscious was working its angles, I wasn't just sitting on my thumbs.

I interviewed and was offered the job of Assistant Director of Football Operations and Recruiting Coordinator.

At the rehearsal dinner for my wedding, I announced to family and friends that I had gotten the job. The day I returned from my honeymoon I was officially a TCU Horned Frog.

The crazy part of the story is it wasn't until years later that I actually thought about the role autosuggestion played in me getting to TCU. Every time I think about that postcard hanging on that bulletin board or that bold statement I made to the rest of the Blinn coaching staff — it makes me smile.

– – –

A cousin of autosuggestion is the law of attraction, which was made famous by the best-selling book *The Secret*. The author, Rhonda Byrne, claims, "as we think and feel, a corresponding frequency is sent out into the universe that attracts back to us events and circumstances on that same frequency."

For example, you will attract events and circumstances that cause you to feel more anger if you think angry thoughts. On the other hand, if you are positive, you will attract positive events and circumstances.

Confession: I struggle with the phrase, "send it out into the universe." It's in direct conflict with my faith.

I'm sharing *all* of this with you — Émile Coué, Napoleon Hill, *The Secret*, etc. because I have designed my own psychological technique, so to speak, taking pieces of each puzzle and turning it into something spiritual.

If you are not a believer, don't panic. This is one of the few times I will put God in the spotlight and share my deep faith.

A couple of my beliefs:

- I believe God is the conductor of this amazing symphony called life not "the universe."
- I believe it's okay to ask God for things you want,

"Ask and it shall be given to you; seek and ye shall find;
knock and it shall be opened unto you." (Matthew 7:7)

Over the years, I've turned my autosuggestion into an intentional prayer. I've tweaked the steps associated with this powerful psychological technique just a little:

Step 1: Figure out what you want.
Step 2: Focus on it.
Step 3: Ask God for direction and guidance to receive it.
Step 4: Believe in your heart He will deliver when the time is just right.
Step 5: Repeat Steps 2-4

In *Think and Grow Rich*, Napoleon Hill encourages people to write a statement expressing their desire for money. He instructs his readers to say exactly how much they want when they receive it, and what they intend to give in return for this money. He writes,

> *Read aloud twice daily the written statement of your desire for money, and to see and feel yourself already in possession of the money! By following these instructions, you communicate the object of your desire directly to your subconscious mind in a spirit of absolute faith. Through repetition of this procedure, you voluntarily create thought habits which are favorable to your efforts to transmute desire into its monetary equivalent.*

Nothing about God.
Nothing about faith.
I realized I couldn't take part in this exercise without those elements. So, I infused Matthew 7:7 — *"Ask and it shall be given to you; seek and he shall find; knock and it shall be opened unto you"* — and I started taking autosuggestion to a new level.

Here's an example of incorporating prayer and autosuggestion, using Napoleon Hill's example on asking for money:

> *Through your direction and guidance, Heavenly Father, I will have $500,000 by (insert date). This will come to me in various amounts from time to time between now and then. In return for this money, I will finally use the gift of writing that you bestowed on me. With You leading the charge ... I believe that I will have this money in my possession. My faith in You is so strong that I can see the money. Because of your love and grace, I can touch it with my hands. I will have this money when I uphold my end of the bargain AND continue to put You first. I am awaiting your plan by which to accumulate this money, and I will follow your guidance once it's received. I will use this money to honor and glorify You. I will provide for my family. I will pay my debts. I will use this money to give back to those less fortunate. In the name of your son, Jesus Christ. Amen.*

– – –

**Author's Note:** As I reflected on my prayer, it felt a little strange to pray for money. But I re-read Matthew 7:7. There is no disclaimer about monetary requests.

As I explained in my prayer, money is a means to an end. That's always been the case for me. I realized to finish this book and continue inspiring others, money is something I need to have. . My family still needs a roof over their head. We need food on the table.

I'm not asking for millions and millions of dollars or to win the lottery. I'm asking for enough money to give this platform and initiative the time and attention it deserves. I'm not asking to accidentally find a sack of money on the side of the road or for someone to write me a check. I'm willing to work my tail off to get it. I'm not asking for this money, so I can sit on the couch and turn my brain to mush with hours and hours of television. I'm determined to use it to help make the world a better place.

I know what I want.

I'm focused on it.

I've asked God for guidance and direction to receive it.

I believe with all my heart and soul He will make this happen when the time is right.

# 7

*There are only two mistakes one can make along the road to truth;*
*not going all the way and not starting.*
*– Buddha*

If you're playing along at home, when I took the job as Assistant Director of Football Operations at TCU, that was job number five in the first seven years after graduating from college. On average, I was changing jobs every 1.4 years.

Yikes!

I'm pretty sure that's not what my dad had in mind when he said, "If you're not happy with what you're doing, go do something else."

Hell, I don't know. Maybe that's exactly what he meant.

The good news is, I hadn't felt like a monumental failure at this point, mainly because I thought I was finally on the right path in college athletics.

The bad news is that path still had many twists and turns to go.

After three years on the TCU Football staff, I worked my way up into athletic administration. I was the first-ever Director of Communications for the TCU Athletics Department. They created the position for me. Pretty awesome, right? It was awesome and not so awesome at the same time. None of us thought the job all the way through, and by 'none of us,' I mean from the athletic director and asst. athletic director and myself. I was in a no-win situation. I'll sum it up by sharing a common statement from my co-workers in the TCU Athletics Department, "What the hell does a Director of Communications actually do?"

One of the most wonderfully great things that happened during that year as Director of Communications was that I was attacked by a nasty bug. It was the entrepreneurial bug, and it stung me directly in the jugular. *I almost said scrotum, but that visual made me cringe too much.*

I left TCU to launch my start-up company — e-Partners in Giving, designed to make memorial giving easy. It was a crazy idea that came to me during a solo camping trip. I remember lying in my tent all night, thinking about the idea of setting up a website to accept online donations for funeral homes. I recall jumping out of my tent as soon as daybreak chased away the darkness. I rummaged through the trashcan at the campsite and found the newspaper I had thrown away the day before. I flipped to the obituaries. I was blown away. This was 2008, and any obituary that mentioned "in lieu of flowers" also asked people to write a check to the non-profit they selected to honor their loved one. In those obits, there was an address for the non-profit to mail them a check.

I thought, *I don't even know where my checkbook is, not to mention a stamp.*

I saw a tremendous opportunity for online giving, but the timing wasn't right, so that didn't work out either.

Statistics show that the average person can expect to change jobs five to seven times in their lifetime. I was about to embark on a run of different jobs to crush *average* and start approaching legendary status. Actually, the adjectives "preposterous" and "ridiculous" might be a better description for the next three years of my professional life.

Here's a quick recap. After graduating from college in 1997, I:

- ○ worked as a newspaper designer at two different newspapers
- ○ served as a college admissions counselor
- ○ coached football

- became a football recruiting coordinator
- worked in athletic administration at a major university
- started my own business

I also:

- helped a non-profit tell its story through marketing
- became a consultant
- worked at an advertising agency

I had an impressive stack of business cards with my name on them. I always wondered if that won me some kind of prize — maybe a lobotomy or a day pass at the closest mental institution?

Just when I thought things couldn't get any more ridiculous, I peeked into the world of oil and gas. I was hired to do marketing for an up-and-coming company in that exploding industry.

The reason this particular job is important to my story — I walked away from a company I whole-heartedly believed in, making more money than I'd ever made because I was not appreciated or valued. I quit without another job lined up because I wasn't true to myself by going to work every day under a cloud of uncertainty and distrust. Please know, when I say "quit," I mean I approached the owners and told them, "This will be my last day to work here. Thank you for the opportunity. I'm sorry it didn't work out."

I grabbed my computer bag and left.

In all my professional twists and turns, it was always important to me to leave a job on good terms *and* make sure I left things in better shape than when I arrived. That was not precisely the case this time, especially regarding leaving on the best of terms. There was no two-week notice or mutually beneficial exit strategy. Obviously, there was not a going away party.

I wanted to include all of this in *Tacos and Chocolate* because it was one of the least proud moments of my life and the proudest thing I've ever done.

I had to walk away, and I had to do it immediately.

A friend of mine put it best, "They didn't deserve you."

Even though she made it sound like I was breaking up with a controlling, self-righteous bitch of a girlfriend, she was right.

If I had gone to work one more day, I would have been a hypocritical glutton for punishment.

Was it easy to walk away? Hell, no!

Before my immediate exit, my heart beat out of my chest as I stared at a picture of my wife and son. My emotions ranged from sadness and anxiety to utter terror as I continuously asked myself, *What the hell am I about to do?*

Then it happened — a whisper from God. I received an e-mail from a friend that simply said:

> *Here's a reminder in case you need one ... "As our pastor closed us in prayer, I told God that I feel like I AM living 'full throttle' and I expressed my gratitude. Thanks to my faith in Him – I'm able to live boldly without any fear. (Not reckless...just boldly.) I'm able to take risks. I'm able to chase my dreams. I'm able to love with all my heart. I'm able to be the best husband, brother, son, and boss that I can be."*

My earnest response to my friend's email was, "Wow! Who wrote that?"

"You did, nerd! In a blog post in 2009," was my friend's response.

The message spoke directly to my racing heart, but being reintroduced to my thoughts and words was even more profound. My fear and apprehension were quickly replaced with confidence.

Before I received that e-mail, I was taking a leap of faith, clueless about what I would do next, but three *very* simple words gave me the courage to embrace my future: *You. Did. Nerd.*

It was a welcomed slap across the face. At that point in my professional life, I *finally* recognized I needed to leverage the gifts God had blessed me with and inspire others through my writing and speaking. It was time to be true to myself and help others do wonderfully great things.

Here is the letter I wrote to the owner of the company I worked for. I handed this to him right before walking out the door.

*Dear (name removed to protect the guilty):*

*I just want to thank you for this tremendous opportunity – to briefly be a part of your incredible vision. Even though this business relationship did not work out, I hope you know how much I believe in what you are trying to do. I've said this to MANY people (family, friends, random people in the community): I definitely drank the "Kool-aid" and was ready and willing to help take you where you wanted to go.*

*What happened?*

*I simply wanted to be a legitimate part of the team. I thought my experience and skill sets could truly help you accomplish your goals. After several conversations over the last two months, I realized that you were unable to facilitate that need/ desire.*

*You asked me on several occasions to be a "team player" – pick up the slack where necessary. And even though I was hired to tell your story in the role of marketing and communications, I was willing to adjust on the move since I believed in what you were doing. The most recent request – splitting my time and energy in other departments – definitely caught me off guard. However, my decision to be proactive with an "exit strategy" had nothing to do with the request and everything to do with how it was handled.*

*From my initial meeting, to my earnest request to be a more integral part of the team, I was disappointed. But my biggest frustration came when we were discussing the details of my new role within the company. The fact that my meeting was scheduled at the exact same time as a singing birthday telegram was unprofessional and disrespectful. It was a complete and utter joke.*

*I tried to push it aside. I tried to let it go. I couldn't.*

*BUT with all that in the rearview mirror, my sit-down meeting with you this morning was going to be the determining factor. You only gave me 10 minutes and that was enough time to make me realize that this wasn't going to work out.*

*I wish you the best of luck. You ARE going to do wonderfully great things. I encourage you to be flexible with the "structure" of your company and focus on the strategy and the people. Those two things will take you where you want to go.*

*Please don't ever forget where you came from and who you are – never, never try to be someone or something you're not.*

*Thanks again,*
*Drew*

– – –

I have one more quick story before I talk about going over to the dark side and working in the family business. This is a blog post I wrote when I had lost my balance on that metaphorical tightrope of holding on to a dream and my responsibility of putting food on the table. This blog post exemplifies my professional journey.

The following will be a humorous way to get to the heart of my story, where I truly started living on purpose. I wrote this back in 2009 when I walked away from my entrepreneurial endeavor, but I could have written it many times over the years.

The name of the post, which was published on May 7, 2009:

### Ever Had To Clean-Up Puke? I Almost Did!

It's no secret that I'm looking for a part-time job.

I haven't announced it to the world by renting a billboard on I-35 or buying a 30-second spot during *The Biggest Loser,* but I've posted Tweets about it and mentioned it on Facebook.

And, of course, everyone knows what that means...

HELP ME!

I am still very much committed to e-Partners in Giving, but I made a promise to my wife that we would never have to be weekly plasma donors in order to pay our mortgage. With our young company still trying to get legs, I have reached the point where it's time to keep that promise.

Break out the want ads, start pounding the pavement ... I'm officially looking for a job, just like I did my sophomore year of high school *(shout out to Little Caesars Pizza; thanks for giving a dorky 16-year-old a chance.)*

A lot of people have asked me, "What do you want to do?"

*Cue the intense desire to throw-up.*

OR an even more vomit-inducing inquiry, "What are you willing to do?"

*Yep ... there was a little splash of puke in my mouth ... OK ... I swallowed it ... no harm, no foul.*

Seriously, I do have a few parameters about re-entering the real world:

- No retail *(the mall is Satan's den)*
- No fast food, even though Kevin Spacey rocked the house when he worked the drive thru in *American Beauty*
- Nothing over 40 hours a week *(Reminder: still committed to making e-Partners work)*

- ○ No pyramid schemes *(I was actually approached by someone when I first started this search)*

Over the last couple of months, I have filled out applications and/ or inquired about the following positions *(responses OR lack of responses noted in parentheses):*

- ○ Sports Program Director at YMCA *("We'll be in touch.")*
- ○ PT Activity Coordinator for Non-Profit Community Center *(No response)*
- ○ Radio Producer for 105.3 The Fan *(Website: "Your application has been received.")*
- ○ Social Media Specialist / Social Networking Coordinator at Texas Research Institute *("...unfortunately your background does not meet our current requirements.")*
- ○ "Love Movies? Articulate? Great opportunity ..." *(No response)*

With my confidence in the gutter, I was ready to do something radical. I was close to completely redoing my resume, removing any important titles, making my master's degree disappear, and putting Little Caesar's back on there.

Then I got an e-mail from a friend regarding a job opportunity. *(Awwww, the power of Facebook.)* It was a forwarded e-mail, and her only comment was,

You did say anything ... and part time...

The job: Carpet cleaning.

Despite frantically looking for a barf bag, I ran through my parameters — no mall, no French fries — Why not?

My response: "I'll do this in a heartbeat ... What do I need to do to make this happen?"

*Don't throw up! Don't throw up!*

My friend sent me the contact information of the carpet cleaner, who she knew through a friend of a friend's second cousin, or something like that.

After the initial contact, the carpet cleaner inquired about a resume. I sent it with no Little Caesar's or Toys 'R Us listed.

*Are you familiar with those enzymes released in your mouth right before you chunk? Cue 'em!*

Can we set up a phone interview? the carpet cleaner asked.

"Anytime" was my quick response.

*Cue intense dry heave.*

A couple of days later, we spoke for twenty minutes on the phone.

"Do you like manual labor?" he asked.

"Like is a strong word, but I don't mind it," I said.

"What kind of pay are you looking for?"

"Obviously a lot, but I'm thinking there is probably a ceiling for carpet cleaning – ironically enough." I giggled and was proud of my job-related humor.

"I see you have your master's degree. Would you have a problem being an assistant?"

"Ummm ... have you ever seen American Beauty? I'm looking for the least possible amount of responsibility," I said.

"What?"

"Never mind. No, I don't think my educational background would impact my ability to clean carpets."

"We'll let you know. We would want this person to get started next week."

"Do you guys ever have to clean up vomit?"

Days passed.

I started sharing this opportunity with friends and family. I was coming to grips with my destiny.

Another day passed.

Then I got the e-mail...

They decided "to go a different direction."

What? I'm not even good enough to clean carpets? I'll show you! Where is my vacuum cleaner? Wait ... where was the nausea?

Why didn't I smell burning feathers extinguished by bile anymore?

Where was my urge to find the closest toilet and give it a bear hug?

After I turned off my vacuum cleaner in mid-stroke, I realized that was the best e-mail I'd ever received.

I stopped, closed my eyes, and prayed. "Thank you, God. I'm following you, and I appreciate you keeping me out of the carpet cleaning business."

With a new sense of purpose and direction, I wrapped the cord around the vacuum cleaner. I put it back in the closet, walked to the computer, and worked diligently on e-Partners in Giving for the next several hours.

*Not a single urge to throw up.*

# 8

"Living each day as if it were your last
doesn't mean your last day of retirement on a remote island.
It means to live fully, authentically and spontaneously
with nothing being held back."
– Jack Canfield

When I walked away from that toxic job in the oil and gas industry, that's when I put pen to paper and realized how many jobs I had after graduating from college.

At first, I looked at this so-called accomplishment as a monumental failure. I felt like a bona fide loser and asked myself self-defeating questions. The main one, "What the hell is wrong with you?"

Then the smoke cleared, and my confidence returned.

I embraced my new role as a retired stay-at-home dad and kept my heart open for my next opportunity or adventure. I wrote more. My unofficial title on LinkedIn was "Retired Stay-at-Home Dad, Trying to Change the World One Blog Post at a Time."

My wife hated that. I think it was the "retired" part and not that I was a stay-at-home dad.

Real quick, here is my take on being retired.

When I got out of that toxic working environment, my wife and I put together a game plan, making her the official breadwinner in the family. I could have steamed milk at Starbucks or stocked shelves at

Costco, but I opted to assume the distinguished title of *Mr. Mom. (Great film ... "Are you crazy? You don't feed a baby chili!")*

I did that for almost six months, and it was a wonderfully great part of my story. My favorite title has always been — and always will be — Dad.

When I would tell friends and family I retired, they looked at me like I was certifiably insane. Every once in a while, there were hyper-dramatic questions, like, "Are you *sure* you're doing okay?"

It was the responses I received from people I had just met — shock, bewilderment, and even jealousy — that helped me formulate my explanation of retirement.

Being retired simply meant that I did whatever the heck I wanted. That basic concept gets lost in some of the myths surrounding retirement:

- I did not sleep in until 11:30 a.m. every day.
- I was still making money.
- I was still active.
- I was not just sitting around waiting for death to knock on my door.

And most importantly:

- I was still relevant.

I had a lot of conversations about retirement after I clocked out of the real world. Some of those discussions were inspiring, while others were tragic.

I remember a story about a gentleman who was retiring after thirty-five years at the same company. He was going to use his pension to chase his real dream of making music.

Awesome, right?

Over the years, I've talked to other people clueless about the next phase in their lives.

"Congratulations on your retirement!" I would say.

"Thanks?"

"What's going to be your next adventure?" I'd ask.

"I have NO idea. Find a hobby, I guess," they would reply.

That has always made my heart break.

I had another conversation about retirement that made my head spin. It was with an older gentleman who was terrified of that word and the concept of retirement. He refused to embrace it.

He said, "I still have a lot of things I want to do." In his mind, retirement meant he was done, finished, caput!

Saying you're retired, or being retired, does *not* mean sitting in the recliner waiting for the Grim Reaper to stop by with a tuna casserole and a lease-to-buy casket catalog.

It's about doing what you want to do.

Maybe that *is* going into an office from eight to five every day or sitting in front of your computer for eight hours. If your job fires you up, and you love going to work, why would you ever stop? Why would you retire?

Unfortunately, so many people work forty to seventy hours a week, doing something that repulses them. Then they *might* spend the rest of the week doing something they enjoy or love, assuming they have the energy left to do so. These same people watch the calendar — year after year — and pray for the day they can walk away.

I simply turned that traditional life diagram upside down.

I spent time with my son.

I only engaged clients I genuinely loved working with. (*When I had time to work, I was doing marketing consulting.*)

I focused on my crazy idea of inspiring people to live on purpose.

I wrote.

Was I getting rich? Nope.

Did I love getting up every morning? Absolutely. I also loved being in control, and I loved planning the next adventure. As weird as it sounds, I loved trying to make financial ends meet.

Here is one more recent conversation I had about retirement. I was working while at a local coffee shop when someone asked me what I was doing.

"Writing a communications plan for one of my clients," I responded.

"I thought you were retired," she said with a scoff and a slight grin, implying she had caught me in the middle of a lie.

Just like many of people, she didn't understand *my* definition of retirement. She didn't get it!

Retirement is *not* a chapter of your life you enter based on age or years on the job. It's a way of life. It's a mindset. It's a wrench in the status quo.

It's doing what you want to do.

In his book *The 4-Hour Work Week*, author Timothy Ferriss shares a powerful story to support my argument. I have referenced this story countless times since I started living on purpose.

You may have heard this story before, or a variation of it, but it's worth hearing or reading again. Especially if you're working a job you hate, simply counting down the days until you can retire.

Here is the tale of the Mexican fisherman:

> *An American investment banker was at the pier of a small coastal Mexican village when a small boat with just one fisherman docked. Inside the small boat were several large yellowfin tuna. The American complimented the Mexican on the quality of his fish and asked how long it took to catch them.*
>
> *The Mexican replied, "Only a little while."*
>
> *The American then asked why didn't he stay out longer and catch more fish? The Mexican said he had enough to support his family's im-*

*mediate needs. The American then asked, "But what do you do with the rest of your time?"*

*The Mexican fisherman said, "I sleep late, fish a little, play with my children, take siestas with my wife, Maria, stroll into the village each evening where I sip wine, and play guitar with my amigos. I have a full and busy life."*

*The American scoffed, "I am a Harvard MBA and could help you. You should spend more time fishing and with the proceeds, buy a bigger boat. With the proceeds from the bigger boat, you could buy several boats. Eventually you would have a fleet of fishing boats. Instead of selling your catch to a middleman, you would sell directly to the processor, eventually opening your own cannery. You would control the product, processing, and distribution. You would need to leave this small coastal fishing village and move to Mexico City, then LA and eventually New York City, where you will run your expanding enterprise."*

*The Mexican fisherman asked, "But, how long will this all take?"*

*To which the American replied, "15 – 20 years."*

*"But what then?" asked the Mexican.*

*The American laughed and said, "That's the best part. When the time is right, you would announce an IPO and sell your company stock to the public and become very rich, you would make millions!"*

*"Millions – then what?"*

*The American said, "Then you would retire. Move to a small coastal fishing village where you would sleep late, fish a little, play with your kids, take siestas with your wife, stroll to the village in the evenings where you could sip wine and play your guitar with your amigos."*

I had become a Mexican fisherman.

# 9

*Be careful not to choke on your aspirations...*
*– Darth Vader*

As I was writing this book, I thought long and hard about the next chapter in my life. More importantly, I thought about the decision-making process to move on from being a "Retired Stay-at-Home Dad, Trying to Change the World One Blog Post at a Time."

All I can remember was keeping an open heart for my next opportunity. There were many discussions and prayers before I jumped head-first into the family business.

After having eleven jobs in the eleven years since graduating from college, having a bachelor's degree in mass communication and journalism, and having my master's degree in educational administration, I became a residential real estate agent.

If your response is not "WTF?", you are in the minority, especially amongst my family and friends.

This appeared to be a random career shift, even for me.

But it wasn't. Real estate was my family's business. My dad was a long-time real estate broker. My grandfather founded one of the most established real estate agencies in Dallas. My aunt and uncle were now running my grandfather's company, and even my cousins were involved in the business.

Real estate was in my blood.

When I decided to get my license, I told people that I felt like Luke Skywalker, going over to the dark side. While that might carry a negative connotation, I was excited and thrilled. At that juncture of my life, I firmly believed everything I had done over the past eleven years — every job, every experience, every life-lesson — had prepared me for that opportunity. I felt like there were four key philosophies I had embraced and fine-tuned over the years, preparing me for the most profound moment of my life.

- Keep Learning
- Communicate! Communicate! Communicate!
- The Power of People
- Never Stop Giving Back

## Keep Learning

Jobs that emphasized this: every job I've *ever* had!

The day I graduated from college my grandfather shared his secret to success with me. He told me to never stop learning. He gave me a journal explaining why this was so important.

I've tried to apply that to every job I've had. The best example is when I dropped what I was doing to be a college football coach. I felt like the more I knew, the better I would be.

## Communicate! Communicate! Communicate!

Jobs that emphasized this: newspapers, coaching, recruiting, ad agency

Solid communication skills are vital in today's world; that's regardless of whether you're a doctor, teacher, mechanic, or ... real estate agent. If you don't know how to communicate with others, you are at a tremendous disadvantage.

What I learned on my *legendary* career path is that there are many ways to communicate, and not everyone receives or responds to the same message the same way. It's about knowing your audience, having a point, and being passionate about what you're writing or talking about. It's also about knowing when to shut your mouth and listen.

## The Power of People

Jobs that emphasized this: coaching, business owner, ad agency, oil and gas

The old cliché, it's not what you know, it's who you know, is true. I think this philosophy has lost a little of its luster because people throw it around so much, but it's still true. The people you know — friends, family, or acquaintances can and will take you where you want to go. They will open doors for you that you didn't know existed. If they can't open those doors, they can introduce you to someone who will.

## Never Stop Giving Back

Jobs that emphasized this: business owner

When I started e-Partners in Giving, the company was designed to make memorial giving easy. I quickly adopted the mantra of "Never stop giving back." I realized that if I was constantly asking people to give back, I needed to walk the walk.

For those who know me well — or just stalk me on social media — you know that mantra changed my life. Whether it was being a Big Brother through the Big Brothers Big Sisters program, volunteering at the homeless shelter, or planning a Day of Giving Back — I wanted to help other people.

- - -

At the time, I thought real estate checked all the boxes for me. All the professional philosophies I had adopted and developed were finally being maximized. It took eleven long years after college to fine-tune that game plan and prepare me for that opportunity. God waited for just the right moment to whisper, "Real estate ... dark side ... you ... *do it!*"

Before that, he knew I wasn't ready.

The crazy part of the story, I honestly thought I had found my calling. I was able to help people and potentially make more money than I ever had.

The craziest part of the story ... I hated real estate.

Not at first, but eventually, the greed of the profession started to beat me down. I thought *everyone* was greedy. The buyers. The sellers. Other agents. It was slowly crushing my altruistic heart and soul. I loved helping people buy and sell houses — finding their dream home or starting a new adventure in their life — but it seemed like it always came back to money. It completely jaded me.

No one respected my time, either. I explained to every client, and potential client, that my wife was a flight attendant. So when she was working, she was gone. I also explained we had two small kids. I would tell them, "My schedule is nuts because my wife actually serves nuts at 37,000 feet, *but* if you give me twenty-four hours' notice, I can make anything happen."

Most of my clients didn't seem to care about my situation. They wanted me at their beck and call. They quickly forgot my dad joke about my wife slinging peanuts on an airplane. "We *have* to see that barndominium on twenty-five acres that is $100,000 over our budget! Right. Now."

I'm grateful I temporarily ventured down the path of real estate because it opened the most random door for me and changed the trajectory of my life forever.

It also helped get me out of the concrete jungle.

I grew up in South Dallas. Duncanville, to be exact. After I got married, we lived in Fort Worth for more than ten years. Don't forget about Houston, the capital of all concrete jungles.

The bottom line: I was tired of city life.

My parents lived in Rainbow, Texas. They moved out of the Dallas/
Fort Worth Metroplex to be closer to my mom's folks, who had land on
the Brazos River. What began as a weekend place for my grandmother,
grandfather, and great aunts turned into their primary residence toward the end of their lives. As kids, we'd spend weekends and holidays
at the farm.

When my grandparents got older, my mom and dad moved from
Duncanville to help Mimi, Grandfather, and The Girls manage the
forty acres. They built a house, starting a new chapter for me, my sisters, and our families. It was a quick getaway from the rat race.

After my grandparents and great aunts all passed away, my mom
bought out her three other siblings' shares. They didn't want to keep
the property, and Mom and Dad had lived in Rainbow for several years.
It had become their home. My folks also had grand visions of turning
the main house into a retreat center for family reunions, church groups,
and corporate gatherings. They also wanted to put a couple of cabins
on the property and rent them out.

That's what they did.

As they both entered retirement, Brazos House Retreat was born.

I remember when I decided to move to the country. My family and
I were spending the weekend in Rainbow, and my dad needed to make
a run into town for some feed for his animals. Brazos House Retreat
had turned into a zoo. Not literally, but my parents had animals everywhere. They had longhorns, goats, chickens, two mules, two dogs,
three barn cats, a duck, a handful of donkeys, and a pig *(shout out to Fatsy
Cline)*. At one point, they even had three alpacas.

Trips to the feed store became a regular thing for my father. On this
particular weekend trip to the country, I tagged along. We took the
farm truck — my grandfather's old beat-up Dodge — into Glen Rose.
We went to Sexton's Feed, which was just east of the historic square.

After our purchase and and the guys loaded our cow pellets and
chicken scratch, my dad was shooting the shit with them like they had
known each other since high school. We made a couple of other stops

around town, and Dad would stop and talk to people every place we went.

I saw small-town life firsthand. It was refreshing.

When we got back to the property, as I helped my dad move the fifty-pound bags of feed, I thought, *How much longer is he going to be able to do this?*

That question got my wheels spinning and ultimately got the ball rolling to get my family and me to Rainbow. The fact I was a real estate agent at the time made the potential move easy. I could simply move my license under a different broker.

It's important to know that my wife wanted no part of this move. Zero. Zilch. Nada. She grew up in the country and vowed never to return. After moving away from Waller, Texas, she had anointed herself a "city girl."

The thought of moving to Rainbow, Texas, made her curl up in the fetal position and cry. Now, it's also important to know Rainbow, on the outskirts of Glen Rose, is only an hour outside of Fort Worth. It's not on the dark side of the moon.

Tanya didn't care. She was terrified her kids were going to live a sheltered, hillbilly life.

But I *was* able to talk her into a trial run.

After going to the feed store with my dad and playing several rounds of "What If We Moved to the Country," we temporarily relocated to Rainbow, Texas.

Yeehaw!

I say "temporarily" because it was just a two-week test to see how we enjoyed living outside the city. My evolving vision was to build a house on my parents' farm and help them manage the forty acres and their post-retirement endeavor with Brazos House Retreat. I would have no problem being a real estate agent in Glen Rose.

Radical honesty: I was tired of city life. I wanted to trade it for gardens, livestock, and tractors. I wanted — and needed — the Metroplex to be in my rearview mirror. I was 98 percent sure I wanted to move.

That two-week trial run was expected to knock out my two percent of doubt.

This is how our first couple of days on the farm went:

- I cleared land for our possible new house. This entailed using a chainsaw and burning anything I cut down.
- I used the tractor to pile my wood.
- Tanya and my son, Crash, harvested onions, green beans, and beets from the garden.
- We all gathered eggs and herded the chickens.
- We gathered rocks.
- We kept tabs on the new baby longhorn.

Yee-Haw! *(Please don't insert any implied sarcasm ... because there is none. In my eyes, our first forty-eight hours of country living had been nothing short of perfect.)*

The part I loved the most was that I felt like it was a bona fide, no sugar-coated, high-octane adventure.

On day one, I almost slipped and fell into the fire pit *(it would have been certain death)*, I got the tractor stuck, and my lower extremities turned into an all-you-can-eat buffet for the local chiggers.

All part of the adventure!

Just like the snakes, scorpions, fire ants, mosquitoes, the mesquite thorns, and the cactus were all part of the adventure, too.

I'm not a masochist, but all those annoyances faded away when the hush fell over the countryside at dusk. The bugs and critters? They didn't matter anymore as the night sky settled over us with stars so bright they would make you dizzy.

I couldn't get that in the city, and that's what I wanted.

I wanted to be the master of my own countryside universe.

No more running around just to be running around.

No more chasing the dream, or my tail, in the city.

No more pretending balance exists.

In my mind, nothing said all of that like a well-oiled chainsaw and a tractor.

By the way, here's how day one played out: I avoided a charred demise, I got the tractor unstuck, and some clear nail polish took the sting out of my chigger bites. None of that stuff mattered as I drank a cold beer and watched the sunset from the patio.

Later that year, we officially moved to Rainbow, Texas.

# 10

*Take a chance!*
*All life is a chance.*
*The man who goes farthest is generally the one*
*who is willing to do and dare.*
*– Dale Carnegie*

Discuss looking good naked ... *check.*
Share about my conversation with Patrick
*(a.k.a. Crazy Joe) ... check.*

Talk about being sexually abused as a kid ... *check.*

Admit to almost cleaning carpets with a master's degree ... *check.*

Disclose how I tricked my wife into moving to the country ... *check.*

I think this is going exceptionally well.

I know. I know. I still haven't explained the tacos or chocolate part of this book. I don't think I've talked about food or nutrition at all.

Reminder: It's not a diet book.

Hopefully, at this point, you realize it's a lifestyle book. It's about mindset. It's about a way of life. The title – *The Tacos and Chocolate Diet* – was designed to pique your interest so you would read the book. Who doesn't love tacos or chocolate?

Back to my story.

We had just moved to the country. I was starting to hate real estate, but the thought of changing jobs again made me want to throw up. I felt like a complete loser. Not really. But kind of.

Then it happened. God brought a radio station to Glen Rose, Texas. It was a nice couple *(shout out to Julie and Mike Greene)* who were launching 95.3 KOME, but it seemed like divine intervention. Why? Because we're talking about Glen Rose, Texas, which has less than 3,000 residents. It's small. It's the only incorporated town in Somervell County, the second smallest county in Texas. If you consider all the people who live outside of town — like the fine folks of Rainbow, Texas — there weren't even 10,000 people in greater Glen Rose.

My point: I never dreamed, in a million years, I would hear the phrase, "They're starting a radio station here." I thought it was a joke.

It was very real.

My new broker was the person who encouraged me to go to lunch with the "radio people." He probably thought it was a solid real estate lead, but it legitimately altered the course of my life.

We ate at the Green Pickle, just off the historic square in downtown Glen Rose. I remember the exact booth we sat in. I told them about my degree in journalism. I shared that I had eleven jobs in eleven years, including stints in the newspaper industry and as a college football coach. I can't remember if I told them real estate was starting to make my butt bleed, but there's a great chance I did.

Most people would have thought, *This dude is a professional train wreck.*

Not Julie and Mike. I guess they were impressed by my charm or how I ate a green chile burger because they offered me a job. Right then and there. They wanted me to do news and sports on their morning radio show. When I explain to people how all this played out, I jokingly say I didn't even let them finish asking the question.

"Would you like to do news and sports on our morning..." Mike didn't get to finish his question.

I excitedly interrupted with a, "YES!"

Here is the crazy part of the story. People of faith would call it a "God thing." That lunch meeting at the Green Pickle wasn't a job interview. I didn't dust off my illustrious six-page resume and bring it with me that afternoon. I thought it was just a "welcome to town" lunch. In hindsight, I guess I was hoping I could help them buy a house when they eventually moved to Glen Rose.

Because I have strong faith, I can say this with 100 percent certainty: God had a different plan.

He knew I was destined to be on the radio.

— — —

"95.3 KOME — where country and rock come together."

I remember the first morning we were on the air, broadcasting across six counties — just outside the fifth largest media market in the United States.

I got to the radio station around 5 a.m. I wanted to make sure the news and sports stories I had gathered from across the region were perfect. We went on at 6 o'clock and did the morning show until 9 a.m. It was called "The Wake-Up Crew — with Mike, Julie, and Drew." Since "Drew" rhymed so nicely with "Crew," I figured I had a little job security going into my first-ever radio gig.

I was nervous. Not as nervous as when I read the announcements over the loudspeaker at my son's school, but I stood firmly outside my comfort zone as Lynyrd Skynyrd and Blake Shelton were getting us closer to 6 am. (Reminder: "Where country and rock come together.")

Right before we went on the air, I got some advice from a buddy who had some radio experience (shout out to Brian Brooks). He reached out to me on Facebook Messenger. I guess he saw a post about me jumping headfirst into the uncharted waters of radio. He gave me the most profound piece of advice.

Brian: Don't screw it up.

Just kidding. Brian didn't say that.

He wrote: *Just be you. Be real.*

As soon as I read it, my nerves relaxed, and my anxiety subsided. If nothing else, I could be myself. And that's exactly what I did.

Mike, the owner of the station and the guy running the show, played the National Anthem to kick off the "Wake Up Crew." He did that every morning. I thought it was cool. Over the next three hours, we talked a little and then played some Van Halen. Then we talked a little more and played some Travis Tritt. I read my handful of news stories six times that morning. I read my sports stories three times. I thought that was a little excessive, especially since I was reading the same stories — the same way — every time. But what the hell did I know? I was a radio virgin.

After three hours on the air, probably only broadcasting to a handful of people, Mike signed us off.

Now, let me see if I can accurately describe how I felt after that initial show. It was like someone injected unfiltered adrenaline directly into my bloodstream with a jet-propulsion firehose. I was on a high I hadn't felt in my forty years on planet Earth. Was it a perfect show? Hardly. Was I anointed the next Howard Stern or Bobby Bones after Mike signed us off at 9 a.m.? Nope.

I probably sucked, but I was hooked. I wanted more of *that.*

Give. Me. The. Microphone.

The glorious part of the story: I was going to get to do it again the next day. And the next day. And the next day.

I couldn't believe it. It was surreal. I was co-hosting a morning radio show in Glen Rose, Texas.

– – –

Here was the initial plan with 95.3 KOME — I'd do the morning show from 6 to 9 a.m. Then, I'd go to the real estate office and work.

The way it actually played out was a bit different. I did the morning show from 6 to 9 a.m., and then I'd hang out at the radio station the rest of the day. I spent more time there than I was at the real estate office.

It was fun.

It was exciting.

I could be creative, whether it was show-prepping for the next day or designing graphics for the station's new website.

There was an energy at the radio station. And that's not a slam on Paluxy River Real Estate. There aren't a lot of jobs or offices that can match that vibe. Now, looking back, a lot of that energy was probably in my head. At first, it was just Mike, Julie, and me. After we got off the air, we went to our separate corners of the building. It wasn't like rock stars — or even up-and-coming country music stars — were coming in and out of the radio station all day. It wasn't like we were jumping on the air whenever we had the urge to say something poignant or funny.

I think it was the potential of something magical happening. Example: The local tractor club might bring in their flyer for us to read on the morning show, or a potential advertiser, like Tan Time, might stop by to get an advertising rate card.

Some people would say it was a sad little office — kind of boring.

I loved it! So, I just hung around.

I won't say I cleaned the bathrooms like most stereotypical start-from-the-bottom stories. But I was willing to do anything and everything Mike and Julie needed.

Here was the problem ... they couldn't pay me any more money. Hell, they weren't paying that much to begin with. They made a point to talk to me after we got off the air one morning.

"You're here all the time," Julie said.

"I know. I love it," I said.

"We can't pay you anymore money," Mike quickly interjected.

"I know. I don't care."

"Really?" Julie seemed astonished.

"I know. I'm an idiot."

"Can you start cleaning the bathroom?" Mike joked.

Confession: I always had a plan. I had this plan when I heard a radio station was coming to Glen Rose, Texas. I had this plan when Mike, Julie, and I ate hamburgers at the Green Pickle downtown. I wanted my own show. I can't remember exactly when I pitched the idea to Mike, but it was probably right after the we-can't-pay-you-anymore-money conversation.

Now, I have to rewind my story a little, and I'm going to dedicate the next couple of chapters to get you guys back to this point.

Don't get frustrated by my non-linear narrative, littered with flashbacks and prefaces to the preface. *Shawshank Redemption* did that. So did *Usual Suspects*. And those are great effing films!

This will all make sense when this book becomes a *New York Times* bestseller, or I win a Marconi, an obscure radio award no one outside of the industry has heard of.

Radio has been my yearning since high school when my buddy Paul would bring his DJ equipment over to my house. He would set it up for days at a time in our living room. I have no idea why Paul would do this, but I never complained. To the complete annoyance and frustration of my parents and sisters, I'm sure I would "play radio" for hours, broadcasting it through the house over Paul's speakers. Ironically, I would pretend I had a morning radio show. It was called "Drew in the Morning." I even had a little jingle I would say over and over again.

That's some cute foreshadowing in my story, but I wanted to take you back to 2008. I was probably between job number six and seven at that point in my professional journey. I wasn't 100 percent sure what I wanted to do with my life. It was before I had kids, so I felt I could continue to embrace my dad's advice of "if you're not happy with what you're doing, go do something else."

During this stretch, I started writing again.

I summoned the old me, a long-haired, narcissistic journalism major, who wrote a weekly column for the school newspaper.

# 11

*Desire is the starting point of all achievement, not a hope, not a wish,*
*but a keen pulsating desire which transcends everything.*
*– Napoleon Hill*

In college, my column in the school newspaper was called *A Different Perspective*. I wrote about hard-hitting things like showering in the dark, changing my name to "Love Myers," and channel surfing.

The goal of my column was to get people to think differently.

In 2008, I wanted to accomplish the same thing with my blog.

On May 3 of that year, I unceremoniously launched *Fire and Motion*. I branded it "Drew's Big Adventure in Life, Business, and Giving Back." My first post was about a hut-to-hut bike ride I did in Colorado. It focused on how I developed my definition of an adventure.

I was off and running.

When I wasn't working on e-Partners in Giving, I was writing.

Note: I'm not going to go deep into e-Partners, my failed entrepreneurial stint. It was a crazy idea I had. I started it right in the middle of a recession. After I got a handful of family members and friends to invest in my business, I left my job as the Director of Communications for the TCU Athletics Department. I scratched and clawed to gain traction, working with funeral homes across the country. My goal was to help make memorial giving easier. And I guess I did gain a little momentum, but when my wife got pregnant in the summer of 2009, I became scared. My business wasn't making any money, and I had a baby on the way. That's when I tucked my tail between my legs and returned to the real world.

During all of this, I wrote blog posts for *Fire and Motion.* My first couple of posts revolved around working from home. I also wrote about Dr. Randy Pausch and his book, *The Last Lecture.* I wrote about giving back. I wrote about my first dog *(shout out to Cpt. Augustus Mc-Crae).*

I loved it.

The fact that only three people were reading my blog regularly didn't bother me. Two of those three people were related to me *(shout out to my mom and my sister, Allison)* and that didn't stop me from posting. I was scratching a creative itch that I had ignored for too long.

One other person read my blog *(shout out to Amy Schroeder).* Amy was a longtime friend who I had kept up with on social media. I knew she was reading because she sent me an email about a potential blog fodder. Her email simply said,

*You need to do this and write about it on your blog!*

It was called the Day Zero Project, and it encouraged people to make a list of 101 things that they wanted to accomplish in 1,001 days. It was a catchy phenomenon started by New Zealander Michael Green in 2003. He had turned up the knob on the stereotypical bucket list, putting an emphasis on the 1,001-day deadline.

Here is the explanation from the *Day Zero Project* website:

> *We believe that by making goal setting fun and competitive you can make real progress on achieving your ambitions. Open-ended goal setting (like bucket lists) doesn't work. It's only when you assign a time constraint that your focus and determination kicks in.*

My friend Amy thought I would like this. She thought I could make a list of 101 things to do in 1,001 days, start to accomplish those goals, and write about it on *Fire and Motion.*

Radical honesty: I was skeptical. I thought it was borderline silly. When I'm speaking to a group, my go-to explanation about Amy's initial email is, "It reminded me of one of those chain e-mails — send this to twenty-five people or get eaten alive by crickets."

I don't know why I thought that. I guess it was a little too cute and kitschy. So I just ignored Amy's email, but she was persistent. She wouldn't back down. She reached out again and kept pushing me to do it.

I can remember when I finally relented.

"Damn it! Okay. Okay. I don't want to be eaten alive by crickets!"

I went and re-read the rules. Here they are straight from the *Day Zero Project* website:

> *The Challenge: Complete 101 preset tasks in a period of 1001 days.*
> *The Criteria: Tasks must be specific (ie. no ambiguity in the wording) with a result that is either measurable or clearly defined. Tasks must also be realistic and stretching (ie. represent some amount of work on your part).*

Then, I thought, *Okay. If I actually make one of these lists, what would be on there?*

I brainstormed — No. 1, 2, 3...

Then, the questions and self-doubt swirled in my head. *Will I actually be able to do that?*

No. 12, 13, 14...

*Is that really stretching myself?*

No. 26, 27, 28, 29, 30...

*Is it supposed to be this difficult?*

No. 55, 56...

*Am I really going to do this?*

No. 89, 90, 91...

*Why can't I sleep?*

No. 100...

*Are there enough hours in the day to actually accomplish all of this?*

No. 101

There was no turning back. My list was done. *(Take that, you bastard crickets!)*

My list was all over the map. Some items were big-ticket, over-the-top *(No. 80: Eat a hot dog and drink a beer in every American League ballpark).* Some were silly or small things that I just hadn't done for whatever reason *(No. 47: Eat a double scoop of ice cream ... No. 64: Host a dinner party.)*

Regardless, it was done.

Here are a couple of other things I wanted to accomplish *(this is a good snapshot of my 101 List)*:

No. 8: Use my passport

No. 29: Help build a Habitat for Humanity house

No. 41: Break the 4-hour mark in a marathon

No. 55: Sell something on Craig's List

No. 65: Plant a tree

No. 78: Eat a fried concoction in front of Big Tex
at the State Fair

No. 84: Throw out the first pitch
at a Major League Baseball game

No. 96: Buy a round of drinks for an entire bar

After I finished, I didn't run out and eat a double scoop of ice cream or warm up my arm for that ceremonial first pitch. I put some leverage on myself. I wrote a blog post and posted my list online for the world to see.

My thought process was, *If I'm going to stumble and fall ... all 7 billion people on Earth can watch me do it.*

Then, it was time to start marking things off my list.

# 12

*If you want to be happy, set a goal that commands your thoughts,*
*liberates your energy and inspires your hopes.*
— Andrew Carnegie

Not long after creating my 101 list, I began calling it a "life list." To me, these 101 things I wanted to accomplish in 1,001 days represented living life.

There was a little confusion in everyday conversation, though. No one understood when I said, "I started marking things off my life list."

To help them understand, I told them it was a lot like a bucket list. But I quickly explained why I liked "life list" so much more. The definition of a bucket list is: "things you want to accomplish before you ... kick the bucket." Things you want to do before you die. I didn't like focusing on death. Regardless, most of us think we're going to live forever, so we constantly use phrases like "I'll just do it next summer" or "we'll just do that after we get out of debt," or "all I need to do is lose these fifteen pounds, and I can *(fill in the blank)*."

That mindset is kryptonite to a bucket list. Plus, it's naïve and ignorant to assume tomorrow is guaranteed. It's not. Will you wake up tomorrow morning? Probably. But you can't be 100 percent certain you will.

Long story short ... stop saying, "I'll just do it tomorrow."

It is the worst phrase in the English language, and it's cloaked in bullshit excuses. Those four and a half words are dream killers. I firmly believe they are the primary reason people don't accomplish their goals and fall short of their aspirations. That phrase paralyzes us to do nothing and embrace the status quo.

Similar dream-killing phrases:

- I'll do it next week.
- I'll do it after _____.
- I'll go next year.
- I'll wait until _____.

Instead of attacking life and going after what we want, we fall into the same-ol' same-ol' — foolishly confident there will be a tomorrow. If we knew the exact day we would die, we could throw around the phrase, "I'll do it tomorrow" with 100 percent certainty.

We don't.

Tomorrow is nothing more than hope.

The philosopher Eminem said it best, "The truth is you don't know what is going to happen tomorrow. Life is a crazy ride, and nothing is guaranteed."

Word.

I noticed my new life list — and its 1,001-day deadline — cut through the nonsense and inspired me to take action.

Real quick, I'm not be the first person to coin the phrase "life list." Author Chris Guillebeau refers to it in *The Art of Non-Conformity*. I'm not sure which of us used it first, but I remember reading his book, thinking, *Hey ... this dude talks like me!*

I love his take on this goal-setting exercise. On his blog, Guillebeau wrote, "A good life list is an anchor. It grounds you in your purpose, gives you hopes and dreams for the future, and helps you understand more about yourself."

Yeah, what he said!

One of my goals for this book is to provide hope for a better tomorrow, and this exercise can encourage a better tomorrow for many of us.

In his book *Make Your Bed*, Admiral William McRaven wrote: "Hope is the most powerful force in the universe. With hope you can inspire nations to greatness. With hope you can raise up the downtrodden. With hope you can ease the pain of unbearable loss."

Yeah, what he said too!

– – –

Another reason I called my 101 list a life list is because it included little things I always wanted to do. Most people's bucket lists are full of pie-in-the-sky items, like learning seven different languages, buying a yacht, or building a dream house out of popsicle sticks.

So, after I created my 101 list, put it out there for the world to see, and rebranded it as a life list, it was time to mark things off.

I wanted to focus on one of those little things I'd simply been putting off:

My first casualty was No. 51: "Participate in a wine tasting."

My wife and I attended one in Dallas just a couple of weeks after creating my life list.

Here are a few highlights from the experience:

- Paul, the leader of the wine tasting, referred to himself — in all seriousness — as the "Wine Master." I loved it!
- I tried 14 different wines; some were awesome, while others tasted like astringent.
- I learned certain wines go well with turkey. *(Again ... astringent.)*
- Ritz crackers cleanse your palate between tastes.
- You don't spit out the wine in buckets if you don't like it. There is a bucket, but it's for pouring out the wine you don't care for and emptying your glass after you wash it with water.

○ "Flabby" is an appropriate description for wine. *(FYI: Lacks acidity.)*

○ I purchased a nice bottle of Dos Rojos; the Wine Master described it as "a wine that will put hair on your knuckles."

After we went to the wine tasting, I had a conversation with a buddy of mine. Here is that actual conversation:

"Did you crash it?" my friend asked.

"No," I said.

"Did somebody invite you after they read your list?"

"I think it was just a coincidence."

"Oh ... I thought they felt sorry for you because you hadn't accomplished anything on your list yet," my friend said.

I was offended and inspired at the same time. I was proud of myself for taking action more than anything because I realized early on that taking action was the key to goal setting. Whether you're talking about a life list, a vision board, or your strategic five-year goals; taking action is crucial.

The vision is just the start of the journey. Taking action is just as important. You can have your goals etched in concrete and commemorated with splats of blood, but if you don't take a step toward accomplishing those goals, it's nothing more than biohazard sidewalk art. Even if it's a baby step, such as typing a random search into Google, you have to move intentionally toward your goals, dreams, and aspirations.

Quick spoiler alert: Your goals are not coming to you! You can't sit on the couch, eating Spicy Hot Cheetos, and drinking Mountain Dew in your underwear, just waiting for the Goal Fairy to knock on your door.

The Goal Fairy knocks. "Did someone order a fifty-pound weight loss with a trip to Cabo on the side?"

Spicy Cheeto Guy yawns and scratches his junk, "I thought you'd never get here!"

– – –

After the wine tasting, I wrote about it on *Fire and Motion.*

After I ate a double scoop of ice cream *(No. 47 on my list)*, I wrote about it.

After I sold something on Craig's List *(No. 55)*, I wrote about it.

The wonderfully great part of this story — people were paying attention. They read my blog posts. But the cool part — they reached out to me, letting me know I had inspired them to make a life list of their own. They had bought into the importance of putting *your* goals, dreams, and aspirations in the spotlight.

I started to see the potential impact of this initiative, but it took eating homemade chocolate cake on fine China plates to realize a life list had the potential to be life-changing.

# 13

*Let's face it, a nice creamy chocolate cake does a lot for a lot of people;*
*it does for me.*
— *Audrey Hepburn*

You might be wondering what happened to the radio station in Glen Rose.

Hold tight. I'll get back there. Promise.

Quick reminder *(just in case you're completely lost)*: In my story, they had moved a radio station to Glen Rose, and I was on the verge of getting my own show.

But there's something important you need to know. If I hadn't eaten homemade chocolate cake on fine China plates back in 2009, that radio show would never have happened.

In the summer of that year, I took a trip to West Texas. My friends Dave and Kimbra lived in the quaint farming community of Levelland, just west of Lubbock. I met Kimbra while working in the Admissions Office at Midwestern State University, my alma mater. She was doing the same job for the junior college in Levelland. Colleges and universities from all over would travel around the state, setting up table drapes and inquiry cards to spread the word about their respective schools. We usually set up in the gym or the cafeteria. That's where I was introduced to the term "cafetorium." I'd been in a cafeteria with a stage before — we had one at Hastings Elementary in Duncanville, Texas. I just had never heard "cafetorium" before I was twenty-five years old.

It was a fun job, mainly because of the friends I made on the road. We followed the same schedule, traveling to these high schools across the state together. When we weren't asking high school kids to fill out an inquiry card or answer questions about financial aid packages, the admissions counselors and recruiters from the different schools would hangout. (*Confession: There were a handful of us who were living the rock-and-roll lifestyle, partying our asses off on the road.*)

I made a lot of friends on those long runs across the state. Kimbra was one of those friends.

Years later, she introduced me to her husband, Dave. He quickly unseated her as my favorite member of the Quinn family.

Long story short, Dave and Kimbra turned into longtime family friends, and they fell in love with my life list. They loved it so much, they made their own life list of 101 things they wanted to do in 1,001 days.

On this particular trip to see them in Levelland, our life lists became the focal point of the weekend.

I remember this vividly and share this any time I'm doing a speaking gig.

It was a Friday afternoon. Dave and I were hanging out with the kiddos at his house. Kimbra was still at work. I asked Dave about his life list.

"Where is it?" I asked.

"No clue," Dave said.

"Go find it! Let's mark something off."

Dave left the room for at least ten minutes. I guess his list was buried in his underwear drawer, which blew my mind. I had published mine online. I wanted the world to see it. There is a good chance that Dave had his hidden under his boxers.

I gave him shit about it when he finally brought it back into the kitchen. It was handwritten on a white sheet of printer paper. Despite being hidden away, there were a handful of things marked off.

I scanned his list, searching for something we could accomplish while I was in town.

No. 3: Meet Sir Richard Branson (*probably undoable on the fly*);

No. 65: Go to a Kenny Chesney concert (*that would have been awesome, but Kenny wasn't anywhere near Levelland, Texas, that weekend*);

No. 71: Get a massage (*I guess I could have helped with this, but I don't think that is what Dave had in mind when he put it on his list*).

Then I saw it. No. 23: Bake Kimbra a cake for no reason.

"Let's do this!" I exclaimed.

Dave didn't seem to be on board with my suggestion. He pointed out that they didn't have a cake mix, and we had already cracked open a couple of Shiner Bocks. He also said he was tired. "Nah. Let's just hang out with the kids and enjoy these beers," he pleaded. "It's been a long week."

I pushed. "Get your ass to the grocery store, and buy a cake mix. We're doing this!"

"What about the kids?" Dave asked.

"Hi. I'm a grown-up. I'll watch the kids. Hurry, she'll be home soon."

He reluctantly grabbed his car keys and walked out the door.

When he got back, he got to work. And just for the record — the kids were still alive, and the house was not burned to the ground when he got home.

As he was measuring and mixing, he shared why baking a cake for Kimbra was on his life list. He told the story about how he would bake for her when they were dating in college. After they got married and had kids, he stopped for some reason.

When he poured the cake batter into the pan, I could tell he knew that doing this — right then and there — was important.

He got the cake into the oven in the perfect amount of time because I remember Kimbra walking into the house and flashing a smile driven by curiosity and wonder. The house smelled like a bakery, thanks to the distinct smell of chocolate wafting from the oven.

"What's going on in here," she asked with a smirk.

"I'm making a chocolate cake," Dave said.

Kimbra, still smiling, asked, "Why?"

"It was on my life list. No. 23," he replied.

I just sat there and drank my beer, not saying a word.

She gave him a big hug and thanked him for the sweet gesture. Then — as if she knew Dave would be summoning his inner Betty Crocker that afternoon — she said, "I'm going to mark something off my life list tonight. We're going to eat that chocolate cake off my grandmother's China."

And that's what we did.

After dinner, we ate homemade chocolate cake on fine China plates. Mark it off and mark it off.

It turned into a very cool evening, mainly because of the conversation sparked by our dessert. We talked about our goals, dreams, and aspirations. We chatted about how we could help each other mark things off of our lists.

That conversation made me realize the power of these life lists. It wasn't just about making a list and marking things off; it was about helping other people put their goals, dreams, and aspirations in the spotlight. It was also about taking people on the adventure with you.

I thought back to one of the books that changed my life, *Into the Wild* by Jon Krakauer. It's a true story about a twenty-something nomad named Chris McCandless, who hiked into the Alaskan wilderness and died. *(I'm not ruining the book — it says that on the cover.)*

Before his tragic and premature death, it was always about the next adventure for Chris McCandless. In one of his journals, he wrote, "The core of mans' spirit comes from new experiences." However, during his last days, alone in an abandoned bus in the snow-covered wilderness, he wrote a note next to the following passage from Doctor Zhivago.

*And so it turned out that only a life similar to the life of those around us, merging it without a ripple, is genuine life, and that unshared happiness is not happiness...*

In his dying days, Chris McCandless realized that the experiences he had were extraordinary, but also meaningless because he didn't get the chance to share them with someone else. Next to that passage, he wrote, "Happiness is only real when shared."

Sitting at Dave and Kimbra's dining table, the wheels in my head were spinning out of control in the most wonderfully great way.

Making a bucket list has been called one of the most selfish things a person can do. I wanted to turn that opinion on its head and make it a selfless way of giving back and attacking life.

Truly living an adventurous and amazing life...

Put others first...

Their story...

Their journey...

Inspiring them...

Helping them.

I was finally connecting the dots dancing around in my brain.

Right then and there, with the crumbs from the chocolate cake still on the plate in front of me, I turned my life list into a gigantic thank you note to God. I reminded myself that He is the reason I'm able to live an amazing and inspired life.

I owed it to God to live a bold, adventurous, and intentional life. I felt like I would be insulting Him if I spent most of my time doing the same ol' same ol' or going through the motions, lying on the couch, watching mindless TV, and eating the before-mentioned Cheetos every single day.

That homemade dessert — and more importantly, that realization — started the evolution of my message and my brand.

After leaving Levelland, I felt that the first thing I needed to do was define what it meant to live boldly. Instead of turning to Google or Webster's Dictionary, I wanted to explain what it meant to me.

My definition: *Confidently living the life that you want, identifying what's important to you, and not letting anything compromise that. Never settling — always fighting.*

Notice I didn't use the words reckless, irresponsible, frivolous, arrogant, *or any synonyms of those dangerous words.*

Author Steve Farber amazingly explained this ideal. In his wonderfully great book *The Radical Leap*, Farber explained the difference between ego-inspired audacity and love-inspired audacity.
Farber wrote:

> *Ego-inspired audacity is just annoying, irritating, or even — when taken to an extreme — dangerous. Some people are audacious just for the purpose of drawing attention to themselves, grabbing the spotlight, puffing themselves up, or advancing their own agenda. They have no care or concern about the impact of their behavior or action on anyone else. They're not concerned about anything except their image.*

It was clear to me that is *not* living boldly. But Farber nailed it when he wrote:

> *Love-inspired audacity is courageous and bold and filled with valor. It's the kind of audacity that's required to change the world for the better.*

Greatness!

It was so great — and it impacted me so profoundly — that I ultimately put all my projects and initiatives under a brand called *Defining Audacity.* (*Thanks, Steve Farber.*)

But wait, there's more. This evolution story doesn't stop there.

Then, I learned of the faith-based concept of *relational joy*, which focuses on laying up eternal treasures in heaven, and those treasures revolve around the people we spiritually touch during our lifetime.

One of my mentors wrote:

> *The person saved will surely be full of joy in heaven. He will not envy anyone and will be delighted in every celebration of God's amazing*

*grace. But the person who has poured his life into others will experience those celebrations with the delight of someone who was privileged to partner in that gracious work of God. Such personal investment enlarges our capacity for joy both now and forever.*

Before being introduced to this amazing way of honoring God, I only focused on the short-term rewards — ones that only last during *this* lifetime. I thought the blessings I was spreading now were the most important thing.

As my mentor explained, "This life is just a blink in relation to eternity."

I quickly realized how short-sighted I was. I also recognized the potential magnitude of helping others embrace their goals, dreams, and aspirations. I saw the opportunity before me as a way to help other people write *their* thank you note to God — one life list task at a time.

So six years later, when Mike Greene, the owner of 95.3 KOME, the new radio station in Glen Rose, asked me what my proposed radio show would be about, I knew the answer before he even finished asking the question.

# 14

*If you have the option of painting a picture of your life,*
*why not make it a good one?*
*Envision your future, your accomplishment and achievements,*
*and your God-given-significance.*
*Based on what you know to be true, of course,*
*not on your own sense of pride or unhealthy ways to satisfy your needs.*
*But within the values and dreams God has given you to accomplish.*
*Expect good and pursue it rather than simply going through life*
*without a plan and seeing whatever happens.*
*– Tony Dungy*

My radio show, initially called *Live the List,* was two hours every Sunday night on 95.3 KOME. I rebranded the show after a few months and called it the *Defining Audacity Radio Show and Podcast.* Why the name change? Legal reasons.

The way I sold it to Mike was an uplifting message focusing on putting our goals, dreams, and aspirations in the spotlight. I put together a run of show for him, which included inspiring songs like *Sun Shines on a Dreamer (shout out to Wade Bowen), Live Like You're Dying (shout out to Tim McGraw),* and *Riser (shout out to Dierks Bentley).*

I talked about my life list. I shared inspirational stories I discovered online. I replayed motivational soundbites I found on YouTube.

My tagline: "Inspire people to live a bold, adventurous, and intentional life — using life lists to accomplish that goal." Sound familiar?

Was it good? I don't know.

At first, it was just me yapping the whole time, so it couldn't have been *that* good. But I loved it. Every Sunday night was an adrenaline rush. When people told me they listened and enjoyed it — that was like Nitro Cold Brew injected directly into my adrenal glands.

But I knew the show could be better. That's when I checked my ego at the door and realized my listeners did not want to hear me ramble for two hours every week.

I brought guests on the show. I did phone interviews with inspiring people across the country, like eighty-one-year-old Babs Cominoli. While I was doing my show prep, I read a news article in the *Tampa Tribune* about her skydiving at eighty-one. According to the news outlet, skydiving was the last thing on Babs' bucket list. After visiting with her on the phone and interviewing her for the radio show, I learned that wasn't exactly accurate. She said there was still a lot of living left to do.

I recorded our phone conversation and played the twenty-three-minute clip as part of my two-hour show. I didn't realize it at the time, but that was my first podcast.

After doing the radio show for a couple of months, I realized listeners were missing badass conversations with wonderfully great people, like Babs.

Another great guest was Samantha Siegel, who made a bucket list for her beloved dog, Teenie-Weenie. When Teenie-Weenie was diagnosed with cancer, she was given a short six to eight months to live. Samantha decided her baby had a lot of living left to do, so she made a Teenie-Weenie bucket list. I had a chance to visit with her about their adventures.

I felt everyone needed to hear that feel-good story — not just those listening to 95.3 KOME in the Greater Glen Rose area on that Sunday night.

That's when my podcast was officially born. I took my recorded conversations and put them online. There were no bells and whistles — no sweepers or background music. It was just these random conversations I had with interesting people. They still live out there on the World Wide Web. Just search "Babs Cominoli Defining Audacity" or "Teenie-Weenie Defining Audacity," and you'll find them.

I quickly bought into the notion people listen to what they want to listen to ... when they want to listen to it ... and how they want to listen to it. That is the driving force behind the popularity of podcasts. It's playing to that on-demand world we were starting to live in, regardless of whether it's music, movies, or TV shows.

Audiences weren't huddled around a massive Zenith Console Tube Radio on Sunday evenings, as if I were Pierre Andre, the announcer for the *Little Orphan Annie Radio Series. "Be Sure To Drink Your Ovaltine."*

So, I recorded *everything* — not just every interview, but every show in its entirety. I would do the show live on Sunday nights, record it, and then drop a podcast of the same show the following week.

Then, I wondered why I was going live at all. I realized I could record my entire show in advance, add all the before-mentioned bells and whistles, and then it would play on Sunday nights. And it would sound better because I wouldn't be fumbling all over myself like I tended to from time to time. I could add the polish.

I was also getting better. I put out a better show. A show I was legitimately proud of.

Next, I pitched my shows to other stations.

At one point, I broadcast on four stations across the region — two internet radio stations, a public radio station out of Stephenville, Texas, and my home station, 95.3. Looking back, it was pretty surreal.

I remember being asked to participate in Career Day at Glen Rose Junior High. The coordinator wanted me to tell the students how I got into radio. This was my speech:

"Howdy! I'm Drew. I'm part of the Morning Crew on 95.3 KOME. I also have my own radio show on Sunday nights. I'm supposed to tell you guys how I got into radio ... well, full transparency ... I got lucky! Are there any questions? No? Thank you for having me."

My presentation was a little more engaging, focusing on my eleven jobs in eleven years after graduating from college, but that narrative was pretty accurate. My first morning show was on March 10, 2015. My first Sunday night show was in late August of that same year. In May 2016, it was officially syndicated *(that's radio speak for it was running on another station)*. By the end of the year, I was on those four stations.

Spoiler alert: My show didn't get picked up by stations across the country; not even by terrestrial radio stations in Texas. You couldn't jump into your car and listen to *Defining Audacity*.

So over the next couple of years, I tweaked my show. If I felt like something wasn't working or starting to become stale, I'd make a change. If I got bored, I'd make an adjustment.

I never got away from the overarching mission of the show, which was to celebrate the power of story and inspire my listeners to live a bold, adventurous, and intentional life. Even when I brought a co-host on the show for two years *(shout out to Shauna Glenn)*, and we emphasized entertaining our audience and making them laugh, it still came back to story and inspiration.

As I write this book, my radio show and podcast are going through another rebrand. I'm looking for the right recipe for success. I'm also juggling a handful of other balloons. I used to say I was juggling grenades, but that sounded so destructive; balloons sound whimsical, fun, and doable.

I'm still doing speaking engagements, delivering my message to groups and organizations across the country.

I've started to host and produce community podcasts, allowing cities and towns to tell their story through those who live and work there.

I do a live-audience show where I sit with singer/songwriters and provide an opportunity to tell the story behind their music. I do that in a listening room setting in front of an audience.

I'm also writing this book.

Sometimes, I wonder if it's too much. Based on everything I do, are my mission and vision unclear? Is it confusing?

I've had friends ask me, "What do you actually do?"

I simply thought they didn't slow down long enough to kind of give a shit.

They thought, "I'll just ask him next time I see him."

Here's the bottom line ... it's all about celebrating the amazing power of story.

It took me a long time to realize this, but I am a story seeker. A friend of mine called me that once in passing, and I fell in love with it (*shout out to Justin Foster*).

I provide others the opportunity to share their story with the hopes that these people will also embrace their story. Through my radio show and podcasts, live-audience shows, my community podcasts, and even my speaking engagements, I showcase and celebrate individuals who have given themselves permission to live radically honest lives, pursue their dreams, and live on purpose.

It took me more than forty years and more than eleven other professions to realize this is why I do what I do.

Am I rich? Nope.

Am I famous? Hardly.

Do I live a joyous and fulfilling life? Absolutely.

Do I dread getting up and going to work every day? Never.

Am I happy? I am.

Content? Yes.

Satisfied? Not even close.

# 15

*The nature of impending fatherhood is that you are doing something
that you're unqualified to do,
and then you become qualified while doing it.*
*–John Green*

This is the last chapter focusing on my story. I had to include it because my narrative is incomplete unless I talk about my kids.

Of all the hats I wear and all the titles I've been given, Dad is — and
always will be — my absolute favorite.

I almost don't know where to begin.

I'll say this ... Crash Greer Myers and Ily Anabelle Myers are two of
my favorite human beings on this planet. I love them more than I can
begin to explain in the pages of this book. I think they're funny. I love
being around them. They inspire me to be a better person.

When Crash was born on Feb. 16, 2010, my life changed forever. It
changed in the most wonderfully great way. I remember walking out of
the hospital on the day he was born, and the world seemed clearer. My
blinders had been ripped off. Everything made sense.

The question I kept asking myself was, "How can people look at
their newborn baby and not believe in God or God's love?"

That incredible feeling hit me like a wave on Feb. 16th at 10:39 a.m.
and has only gotten stronger.

Then, there is Ily Belle.

When I found out my second child was going to be a girl, my mouth went bone dry, my palms sweated, and my trigger finger got itchy. I was petrified.

"You'll be fine," people told me to help combat the terror they saw in my eyes.

I would smile through the fear and whisper to myself, "I know. They're right." But deep down, in places I don't like to talk about, I thought, *This little girl is going to be the death of me.*

Well, Ily Anabelle wasted no time giving me my first heart attack. She was delivered via emergency C-section in a flurry of events I appropriately like to describe as "western" – when shit is starting to go down.

After becoming distressed in utero, Ily's birth went from boring to terrifying in seconds.

Before I continue, I want to jump to the end of the story. Everyone needs to know that Ily is doing wonderfully great. As I write this, she's eight years old. She's beautiful inside and out — with a little bit of sass.

However, on the night of July 26, 2013, we thought we'd lost our little girl.

My wife had no trouble giving birth to our son, Crash. It seemed like her water broke, and he popped right out. I barely remember anyone saying, "Okay ... now push!"

It was such an easy delivery; people joked about my wife giving birth to our daughter. My mom, a longtime nurse, said, "When Tanya goes ... she's going to go *fast!*"

I had visions of my wife giving birth in the car on the way to the hospital or me delivering Baby Ily at home with my son's baseball glove and catcher's mask.

So when my wife's water broke while I was three hours away in Austin, I told Tanya, "Give my daughter a kiss. I'll meet her in a few hours."

I canceled my scheduled meetings in Austin and drove as fast as my 2001 Chevy pickup would go back to Fort Worth.

As I was driving 90 mph — weaving in and out of traffic — I smiled and thought *Nothing like a little drama from a stinkin' little girl.*

Confession: I was excited.

When I arrived at the hospital, there was cheerful energy. My giddiness just added to the optimistic anticipation.

My folks were there. My sister and her kids, too.

No Baby Ily, though.

Tanya and the nurses worked hand in hand to ensure I made it back into town before she was born. I was thankful and even more excited than ever.

"Let's do this," I said as I burst into the delivery room.

Well, Ily Belle wasn't ready yet. So hours passed with not a lot of excitement. It was the typical hurry up and wait I'd heard about in the delivery room.

At 10 o'clock that night, I regretfully said, "This is boring."

The next update we received from the nurses at around 10:30 p.m. indicated it would be a *long* night. Tanya was still only dilated to five cm, which meant she probably wouldn't start pushing for a couple of hours.

"I could have driven back from St. Louis," I said with a disheartening smirk as I kicked up my feet to watch the end of the Rangers game.

That's when all hell broke loose.

I don't want to pretend to know or understand what happened in the next six to seven minutes, but it ended with four nurses pushing my wife out of the room at a dead run.

My memory is a little hazy, but I remember snippets of dialogue between the nurses.

"We're going to have to do a STAT C-section ..."

"Are they ready?"

"We've got to go NOW!"

"Hurry! Hurry! Hurry!"

Tanya wasn't receiving any information. I wasn't getting any either. The nurses' extreme sense of urgency and encrypted chatter had made us invisible.

The look on my wife's face was sheer horror. Several days later, she confessed she thought Baby Ily had died.

After the nurses bolted out of the door, leaving the delivery room eerily silent, I turned to my mom — the only nurse I wholeheartedly trusted. I calmly said, "Tell me what's going on, Mom."

"I'm not sure, honey."

With those four and a half words, fear raced through my veins.

My mouth went bone dry, my palms started sweating, and my trigger finger began to twitch.

I didn't know what to do, so I prayed.

Seconds seemed like hours.

Minutes were a lifetime.

More prayers.

There was no one around, which meant no answers, explanations, or updates. The first nurse I saw following the rushed departure was a new face. She wasn't there during the chaos. I was hopeful she had some news, though.

All she said to me was, "You can't stand in the hallway, hon. You need to wait in the room."

When she closed the door to the delivery room behind me, I imagined that's what a prison door sounded like when it slammed behind you.

I wanted to scream at the top of my lungs, but I just continued to pray.

Finally, a nurse with a familiar face came into the room. "Are you Dad?"

With my voice shaking, I said, "I am."

"Let's go!"

I put on a cap, mask, and scrubs as we walked hastily down the empty hallway. We approached a set of double doors, and I said another small prayer before she pushed them open.

The room was bright, brighter than any room I'd ever been in. There were doctors and nurses everywhere, and the sense of urgency was even more intense than before. I was disoriented and confused.

I heard a baby crying, but I wasn't sure if it was my baby.

They sat me next to my wife, who still looked scared. She was lying awake on the operating table. A curtain blocked our view of a handful of doctors and nurses working on her.

I kissed her forehead.

"Where is Ily?" she asked.

"I hear her crying," I said, praying that it was her screaming across the room.

Right then, a nurse calmly approached us. "Dad, would you like to meet your daughter?"

For the first time since I kicked my feet up in the delivery room, I took a deep breath. Her calmness made me feel like everything was going to be okay.

A handful of doctors and nurses checked out our little girl, but they were calm. They provided optimistic feedback and updates, which I appreciated after the communication debacle to this point.

I ran back to Tanya to ease her worried mind. "She's beautiful. You did great!"

I kissed her forehead again.

Joy replaced Tanya's terror. Her eyes began to water. She was still rattled, but her panic was subsiding.

Because of the stress associated with the delivery, Ily had some issues initially catching her breath. She was admitted to the NICU so they could keep an eye on her. Before they wheeled her out of the room, I whispered in her little ear, "Fight your ass off, baby girl. That's how we do it in this family. I love you."

That's exactly what our six-pound bundle of love did. She was in intensive care for less than twelve hours. By Saturday morning, Ily Belle was back in our arms where she belonged. We were still in the hospital, but we were together.

The nightmare of that horrific Friday night was temporarily forgotten.

We spent the rest of the weekend loving our baby girl.

She got to meet her big brother, who loved her immediately. We had a handful of family and friends stop by to see us. The doctors and nurses continued to provide positive updates.

Friday night was the furthest thing from our minds. It seemed like a horror movie that someone else had lived through.

On Monday morning, as people started coming back to work, we found out the seriousness of Ily's birth.

People were fired.

Risk management was on high alert.

A lot of staff were apologetic.

I don't want to pretend to know or understand what went wrong during those six to seven minutes of hell, but I do want to emphasize the power of prayer. Talking to my mom on the phone Monday morning, she said, "It could have been bad. I didn't want to say anything before now."

"How bad?" I asked cautiously.

"If Ily hadn't been as healthy as she was, or if Tanya wasn't as healthy as she was, the baby might have died."

My heart sank, and I closed my eyes. I took a deep breath — exhaling slowly and deliberately, exemplifying my gratefulness.

I finished my conversation with my mom. As I ended the call, I promised myself to never think about it again. My little girl was alive and on the road to being healthy. I vowed to remain grateful for God's blessing and not relive the "what ifs" from the night of July 26, 2013.

– – –

To reinforce my love of being a father, I thought I would share a of couple random blog posts I've written about my kids over the years. Otherwise, I'm going to fill the next pages with "I love them very, very, very, very much."

FYI: If narcissistic fathers annoy you in any shape, form, or fashion ... I'd advise you to stop reading and skip right to Chapter 16.

I originally wrote this blog post – *Three Powerful Words: 'Just Like Daddy'* – in November 2012. Crash was a couple of months away from turning three.

### Three Powerful Words: 'Just Like Daddy'

I've previously written about the parental guidance I've received over the last few years — before, during and after The Boy was born. The salesperson at Hallmark won the gold medal when she said, "It goes so fast... enjoy every minute of it."

For some reason, I was dwelling on her nugget of advice the other day.

It was probably when my son cracked a beer, kicked his feet up, and asked if I thought the Cowboys would cover the spread. OR it might have been the first time he pooped in the toilet without me begging or bribing him with jelly beans.

Either way ... she was right. They DO grow up fast!

So fast!

This humbling realization reminded me of some other parental insight I received right after Crash was born. It revolved around "Life Chapters."

I was having a conversation with a friend of mine who has older children. Her youngest child was about to leave for college, and I asked her about empty nest syndrome.

"Are you worried about it? Are you going to be sad and depressed?" I asked.

My friend said, "Not at all. I've enjoyed every chapter to this point. This is just another one. I'm looking forward to it,"

She was so confident and at peace.

Somewhat rhetorically, I asked, "Chapters?"

"Sure. The newborn chapter was great — new and sweet — but the walking and talking chapters were even better. The pre-school chapter was fantastic, but when they started elementary school ... so fun. The older they got, the activities ... watching them grow into adults ... each chapter has been terrific in its own way," she responded.

"What's been the best chapter?"

"Each one is better than the last. It just keeps getting better!"

Every time I hear "Daddy ... I need you to wipe my butt" these days, I think about these "Life Chapters." I reflect on the amazing journey we've already traveled since Crash was born, and I start to get excited about where we're going.

The newborn chapter — represented by the hundreds of diapers — was awesome. Every day it was something new — a smile, a sound, a unique smell.

The toddler chapter — represented by even more diapers — was remarkable as well. Whether he was learning to waddle around the house, babbling to hear himself babble or finally being able to differentiate me from the dog — it was wonderfully great.

Within these chapters there are sub-chapters, too – like stringing words together *(even if they don't make sense)*, transitioning to a big boy bed and getting brave and adventurous.

All part of the "Life Chapters." All remarkable in their own way.

Like my friend poetically explained to me, though, the current chapter is definitely the best. Here is the present storyline in the Life of Crash:

- The Boy is starting to declare his independence: "I do it myself!" *(That's whether we're changing out the laundry or starting my pick-up.)* His confidence has grown because of this, too. After finishing the task, he'll always declare: "I DID IT!"
- He likes EVERYTHING.

"What's dat?" he asks.
"Dog poop," I reply.
"I like dog poop!" he exclaims.

○ He has the weird knack of finding things that are "just da same." Example: If he sees a picture of a frog, he'll scour the house until he finds every other frog that he's ever seen — pictures, stuffed animals, etc. After 5 minutes, it's like a re-union of frogs — or whatever the object of his infatuation.

BUT ... my favorite part of our current chapter is: "Just like daddy!" *(Hang on ... here comes the narcissism.)*

It doesn't matter what I'm doing, Crash wants to be "just like daddy."

If I'm wearing a blue shirt — The Boy wants to wear a blue shirt.

If I'm mowing the yard — he wants to mow the yard.

If I'm going "teetee" in the potty — he wants to be "just like daddy" and "teetee" in the potty.

There is NOTHING in this world that warms my heart more than those three words.

I know ... I know ... call me vain or self-absorbed, but feel free to use the adjectives scared and/or humbled as well. They are just as applicable. When Crash says, "just like daddy," it's an overwhelming reminder that I have a responsibility as a father to be a positive role model for my son.

That's why I take him running with me.

That's why we go to church.

That's why I love on his mamma in front of him.

Do I want The Boy to do EVERYTHING "just like daddy?"

Ummmm ... negative.

I know I drink too much beer, put too much salt on my food and stay up too late, but now I'm aware that little eyes are watching and I try not to miss a potential teaching moment:

– "Remember, only daddies and mommies drink beer."

– "No ... salt will make your heart stop. How about some pepper?"

– "Daddy is stupid. He SHOULD go to bed at the same time as you!"

– – –

So how in the world do I put a nice big bow on this chapter and tie it all together? *(I've asked myself that question about twenty-six times since I started writing it.)*

Then it hit me.

One of my goals for this book is to inspire others to live boldly, and I decided early on the best way to do that was to share my story. Paint a picture of how I'm able to live a bold, adventurous, and intentional life.

Crash's "just like daddy" chapter inspired me to live boldly.

Why? How?

Because of the incredible responsibility associated with those three words — the decision-making process in my life became crystal clear. When staring down the barrel of a tough decision, the only question I had to ask myself was, "What's the best thing for my family?"

I decided a long time ago that my top life facets were my faith and my family. Everything else was a distant third.

My life hasn't been the same since making that defining decision.

I want people to realize that — especially my son. I can't wait until he embraces his faith and recognizes the importance of family — inspired to be "just like daddy." One. More. Time.

– – –

One more #dadintraining blog post from the archive. My story is irrelevant if you don't understand my love affair with being a father.

I wrote this in December of 2014. It is entitled, *The Ultimate Goal: Seeing Your Kids Shine.* It was after my son played organized soccer for the first time. I was the coach. The story is about how I was tricked into coaching, and why I'm forever grateful that I was.

### The Ultimate Goal: Seeing Your Kids Shine.

I guess I was a little blind-sided by the question:

TEXT: Would you like to coach Crash's soccer team?

It came via text message from a telephone number that I didn't recognize at the time. It surprised me, because I had already indicated that I wasn't interested in the job when we went through the registration process.

When I got to the part of the online sign-up form that inquired about coaching, I thought about it for one second.

Text: Do you want to coach your child's soccer team?

Me: Nope!

My reply text to inquiry No. 2 was a little more thought out and definite: "Not just no, but ..."

Text: We don't have enough coaches. You'll do great.

Me: No thanks.

Text: Please.

Me: I played soccer for like fifteen minutes when I was growing up. I'm not qualified.

Text: We'll give you an assistant who has played before.

Then I revealed a chink in my armor.

Me: When do you need to know by?

I wish I could write, with pure confidence, that my decision to do it was altruistic — my son needed a soccer coach, and I was going to save the day.

That wasn't the case, though.

It was a little touch of guilt — and the fact that I've never backed down from a challenge — that pushed me over the edge.

Me: OK ... dang it ... I'll do it!

Text: Sucker. I knew you would!

Fast-forward to our initial team meeting, which took place after our first practice. Five sets of parents sat on metal bleachers with temperatures pushing 100 degrees. They had just watched me pretend to be a soccer coach for an hour. The six players on the Lions — our prideful team name chosen by my 4-year-old son — ran around the soccer field like wild banshees. They were acting like they hadn't just practiced for 60 minutes.

I stood in front of the parents sweating and nervous, trying to block out the chatter coming from the 4 and 5 year olds running wild behind me.

*"I've never played soccer like that before..."*
*"Are all the practices going to be like this..."*
*"Is he really our coach..."*

I took a deep breath and focused on the parents.

"I appreciate you guys letting me coach your kiddos..."

I knew they could see right through me. They had just sat and watched me herd cats for an hour, and they were thinking the exact same thing the players were saying out loud.

So, I decided that brutal honesty was the best game plan.

"I'm not a soccer coach. I only played soccer for a couple of years when I was growing up. I stopped playing in the sixth grade."

The initial response was wide eyes and one long deliberate breath from every single parent. *(I've never witnessed an actual train wreck, but I'm thinking this is a common reaction from the on-lookers.)*

"I was a football coach for 4 years..."

A couple of the parents actually did the slow blink and dropped their heads. I quickly made each one of them a promise.

"I will come to practice organized, ready and excited every week ... I'll try to make the experience as enjoyable as possible for your child ... I'll be fair ... I'll treat each of your kids like my own — with love and respect.

"My No. 1 goal is for your son or daughter to have fun — if they get a little better at soccer and we win some games, it will be icing on the cake.

"If any of you have tips or suggestions for me, I'm all ears. When they handed me my whistle and clipboard, I checked my ego at the door..."

Confession: I felt good about my preseason pep-talk — especially after I introduced my assistant coach and explained that he actually played soccer through high school.

Fast forward to the middle of the season...

We weren't very good, but the kids were allegedly having fun.

For me, it was a rollercoaster ride. Fortunately, the first practice was an anomaly — it wasn't always like herding cats. Sometimes it was like herding butterflies and/or rabid raccoons.

Confession: After every practice, all I wanted was an adult beverage.

I tried to stay positive, constantly reminding myself that it really wasn't that awful. Our No. 1 objective was to have fun, and I would ask my son after every game if we accomplished that goal.

"I know we lost by twelve goals, but did you have fun?" I asked.

"Yes, sir," Crash responded.

"You do know it's A LOT more fun when you win, right?"

"I'll take your word for it, Dad," he said.

I will say this ... we were getting better. By the fourth and fifth game, we were starting to be competitive, and after I bribed my players with candy if they scored a goal, we started winning games.

Needless to say, I was having a lot more fun as the coach when we weren't getting embarrassed.

I also started having a lot more fun as a DAD!

In game No. 6 of the season, Crash Greer Myers — my pride ... my joy ... my first-born child — scored the first goal of his short soccer career. I can whole-heartedly say that it was one of the proudest moments of my life.

I know ... I know ... it was just a U6 youth soccer game and there wasn't a goalie, but when that ball hit the back of that tiny net, it was magical.

The Boy immediately turned around searching for my validation.

He found it.

When our eyes locked, and I saw the pure joy and excitement on his face, fatherhood finally started to make sense. Right then and there, it wasn't about me anymore — I realized that it was about the success of my children.

He tried to play it cool, but he was overjoyed.

And so was I.

He wanted to score so badly, and he finally did it. I was so happy for him.

I ran up to him *(coaches are allowed to be on the field during U6 games)*, I picked him up and threw him in the air.

"I scored, Daddy! I scored, Daddy!"

"I know you did, brother! I'm so proud of you."

As I set him back down on the ground, my face began to hurt from smiling so much.

I squatted down, looked him in the eye and told him again, "I'm really proud of you, Crash."

He smiled and said with a twinkle in his eye: "Does this mean I get a Ring Pop, Dad?"

# 16

*Yesterday I was clever, so I wanted to change the world.*
*Today I am wise, so I am changing myself.*
*— Rumi*

*S* *hit!*
I have no idea how this book is supposed to end. My story isn't over. I haven't reached the summit, and I'm not on my deathbed.

Real quick ... if I *was* knocking on death's door, I'm ready. My faith is strong, and I've already planned my funeral. Just sayin'.

In 2012, I wrote a blog post laying out the blueprint of my funeral. My interment was highlighted by the singing of *American Pie* (*shout out to Don McLean*) and a rainy graveside service with bagpipes. Can a civilian receive a twenty-one-gun salute? Not asking for a friend. I'm asking for me.

Anyway, my funeral will be awesome, but I don't plan on dying anytime soon.

So, that makes the end of this book tricky.

I decided I should share my recently adopted mantra.

This is a blog post I wrote on May 29, 2020 – during a global pandemic.

### An Empowering Look in the Mirror.

A friend of mine had asked me how everything was going. He asked me if I was doing okay. I responded by saying: "I'm so wonderfully great. I've actually never been better. Things aren't perfect, but they're really effing good."

That was the truth.

Zero bullshit.

I attributed 90 percent of that to self-love and self-care, which I really started putting an emphasis on earlier that year. From working out and reading, to praying, writing, and focusing on my affirmations ... I had been healing and growing since early in 2020. That was physically, emotionally, mentally, and spiritually.

Then came Covid-19, and I turned up the knob.

During all that coronavirus madness, I never let it rattle me. I never got down in the dumps or scared. There were a couple of days that I got pissed off — but it was short-lived. Those streaks of anger lasted about twelve hours, and a little self-love the following morning always gave that fury the middle finger.

I refused to feel sorry for myself. I refused to be a victim. I focused on me in the midst of the uncertainty. I focused on self-care to get me through homeschooling my two kids and living through my own *Groundhog Day*. I focused on self-love to block out the negativity, and the "sky is falling" bullshit being screamed on the TV and through social media.

One of the biggest parts of my self-kindness was reading and listening to audiobooks.

I was introduced to two incredible books: *It Takes What It Takes* by Trevor Moawad and *Can't Hurt Me* by David Goggins. *(Another shout out to my friend Dave Quinn for the recommendations.)* They spoke to my soul, and they both had a lot of takeaways. There was one particular nugget from each book that I decided to adopt. I wanted to share how I incorporated these tools in my self-care repertoire.

Trevor Moawad, a renowned mental conditioning expert and strategic advisor to some of the world's most elite athletes, shared about the time he spent with four-time gold medalist Michael Johnson.

Moawad wrote about the "mantra" that Johnson would say before every race.

It was simple. It was powerful. It carried Johnson to four gold medals and eight world championships.

> Head down.
> Pump your arms.
> Explode.
> I am a bullet.

Moawad's narrative surrounding this "mantra" inspired me to come up with my own — something I could repeat to myself over the course of the day to help me be my best self and "perform" at maximum effort. *(I'm definitely not comparing my daily life to the Olympics, but it is my own race.)* This is what I adopted:

> Eyes on God.
> Others first.
> No excuses.
> I am a warrior - stay in the fight.

Each one has an explanation, but that's for my next book. *(Again, that's called a tease.)*

Now, welcome David Goggins to the story. I refuse to ruin his powerful book and his incredible story, so I'll just say that David Goggins is a badass m-effer. He took the shitty cards he was dealt and single-handedly changed the trajectory of his life. Example: At one point, he weighed almost 300 pounds. Then, he worked his ass off to lose more than 100 pounds and live his lifelong dream of becoming a Navy Seal.

In his book, *Can't Hurt Me*, Goggins offers challenges to his readers. One of those challenges was creating an Accountability Mirror. During a dark time in his life, he used a mirror and Post-it Notes to be honest with himself and hold himself accountable.

I accepted his challenge, writing my "Michael Johnson mantra" on the mirror in my "apartment." *(My apartment is simply that unfinished bonus room above our kitchen. My podcast studio is up there. I work out up there. I paint and write up there.)*

I had to pass that mirror every time I walked in and out of my "apartment." My new "mantra" was in my face, reminding me what I need to do in order to be the best version of me.

In one of these two books — I honestly can't remember which one — the author said, "If you're not getting better, you're getting worse."

— — —

So, how am I going to end this book? I'm going to refer back to Admiral McRaven again. I've decided to follow his lead, from his book *Make My Bed,* to tie a nice red ribbon around *Tacos and Chocolate.*

In his book, he offered ten lessons he learned while he was in Navy Seal training. The chapters are short, sweet, and impactful. I wasn't a Navy Seal, but that could help me. I'm just an average dude, writing a book for ordinary people.

Here are the ten lessons I've developed to help me live on purpose:

1. Get to the point of enough.
2. Be able to sleep in a storm.
3. Make the important things important.
4. Ask yourself "What's next?"
5. Focus on #myonething.
6. Count your wins.
7. Watch how you talk to yourself.
8. Pray like Mr. Rogers.
9. Make one person's day.
10. Do one thing that scares you.

— — —

"Hey! Hold on! Where are all the stories about people losing fifty pounds by simply eating tacos and chocolate?" you might ask.

This isn't a diet book. It's a lifestyle book. It's about taking control of your life right now — not waiting until next weekend, after you lose those before-mentioned fifty pounds, or after the kids are out of the house. It's not about waiting for that perfect moment to make a change or start chasing your dreams.

Spoiler alert: There is no perfect moment.

That is one reason I dislike New Year's Resolutions. I've always been a believer; if you need to make a lifestyle change or kick a bad habit ... just do it! Does it matter if you do it in April, June, or September? If I had to wait until January every year to switch things up, my life would be a mess for *at least* 350 days of the year.

I wrote a blog post in 2009 that referenced Britney Spears. Her New Year's Resolutions for that year were to stop worrying ... and stop biting her nails.

Come on, Brittany, stop doing that shit right now. Don't wait three weeks.

I have never understood the rationale for waiting to make a change.

My longtime buddy, Greg Jones, smoked forever and ever. We met in the fifth grade *(he didn't smoke then)*, stayed friends throughout junior high and high school, and were college roommates. We're still friends today. Throughout high school, college, and our adult lives, I probably asked Greg to quit smoking at least 673 times. He always had a plan of attack and a timetable for me. *(That's a clever way of saying he had a bullshit excuse.)* "I'll stop after I write this paper" or "I'll quit at the end of the semester."

He had the perfect moment mapped out in his mind. Paper done ... Greg Jones kept on smoking. Semester over ... still smoking. Now, Greg did eventually stop, but it took the birth of his beautiful daughter to make it happen. It finally became important to him. Greg eventually got to the point of *enough*, and that is where the magic starts to happen.

Let me explain.

Part II of this book walks you through those ten lessons. My goal is that they inspire you to start living the life you desperately desire.

# 17

Part II: Ten Lessons for Living on Purpose

*Lesson 1: Get to the point of enough.*

I think the most disheartening and tragic phrase in the English language is, "I'll just do it tomorrow." I've mentioned it several times so far in this book, and there's an outside chance you'll read it again before the epilogue.

A few years ago, I was throwing around those four and a half words like a Nerf football, specifically regarding running.

Finally, I was sick of it.

I told myself, "If I make up one more excuse why I can't run, I'm going to strangle myself with my shoelaces." Hell … I wasn't using them for anything, anyway.

That is how my running streak started. My son, Crash, was about to turn one. I weighed more than I ever had before. I was also drinking a lot and eating like I was twenty again. I did not look good naked.

The worst part, I was an excuse machine.

I enjoyed running, but I could give you an excuse why I shouldn't, or couldn't, run in a second.

It's too hot.

It's too cold.

I just ate.

I haven't eaten enough.

I'm tired.

I have gas.

My legs are sore.

It's too late.

I have too much to do today.

I'm too drunk.

Then a friend of a friend (*shout out to Glen*) introduced me to the concept of streak running He had started a streak on two occasions. He ran at least a mile every day for more than a year – twice.

I thought it was admirable, inspiring, and cool. But those three adjectives are not enough to start a running streak. I had to get to the point of enough.

What is the point of enough? It's that moment when you're screaming inside your head, "ENOUGH ALREADY, DAMN IT!"

Spoiler alert: Sometimes, we need help getting to the point of enough. Just like Greg Jones, who held onto his smoking habit until he became a dad.

My son, Crash, helped me get to the point of enough. I refused to be a bad influence on him. To put a positive spin on it ... I didn't want my son to think his dad was a lazy piece of shit. That is why I started my running streak and why I've kept it going. As I'm writing this book, I've been streaking for just over ten years.

This is precisely how I got to that point and screamed, "Enough!"

When Crash was a baby, I took part in a life-changing, personal development exercise. I was encouraged to write myself an inspirational letter about the importance of staying active. I think the American Heart Association put on the event. The organization collected the notes and mailed them out a month later. My letter said:

*Dear Drew ... get your lazy ass off the couch and start being an inspiration for your son. Run!*

After receiving my note in the mail, I started running at least one mile every day.

Why is lacing 'em up and pounding the pavement important to me? Because I know my son is watching.

Is that too rainbows and bubbles? Are you the type of person who needs the research?

Cue the research!

I stumbled upon a great academic article by a student at the University of New Mexico entitled, *What Starts and Keeps People Exercising?*

The author put together a self-regulatory strategy that revolved around the following components:

1. Self-perception;
2. The belief that exercise will improve yourself;
3. S.M.A.R.T. goal setting *(strategic, measurable, attainable, realistic, and timely)*;
4. Specific action.

I thought it captured my running streak beautifully.

I thought I was becoming a soft-in-the-middle excuse monster.

I believed that if I ran every day, I'd look good naked and be a good role model for my son.

My goal: Run every single day — no matter what.

I put on my running shoes and ran.

But there is more to life than just getting motivated to work out or look good naked, right?

In my limited research, I was reminded of Maslow's hierarchy of needs. This pyramid reminds us we need to eat and poop before we can experience intimacy or have the respect of others.

I love the top of the pyramid, which focuses on self-actualization. Those needs include realizing personal potential, self-fulfillment, and seeking personal growth and peak experiences. It's no secret I like to play with these pieces of the psychology puzzle, which — according to Maslow — means the rest of my pyramid is in tip-top shape.

He said, "One must satisfy lower-level basic needs before progressing on to meet higher-level growth needs. Once these needs have been reasonably satisfied, one may be able to reach the highest level called self-actualization."

Yeah – what he said!

I feel inclined to dumb things down a little more than Abraham Maslow. Even though I took psychology in college, I thought it was stupid, and my grade reflected that.

So when my running streak hit the two-year mark, I developed a theory on motivation: You've got to get to "enough" before anything is going to happen.

If you want something badly *enough*, you will go and get it.

If you've had *enough* of something, you will make a change.

If it's important *enough*, you will fight for it.

No excuses!

Sure, there might be external factors involved — like a scary diagnosis from a doctor reminding you that life is short — but you're still reaching *enough*. When a doctor tells a person to lose 100 pounds or they're going to die ... they'll probably drop the weight! Why? Because most people's desire to live is strong *enough*.

Another component to *enough* is reaching your breaking point — having enough of something to make you change. That moment when you're completely fed up.

On day one of my running streak, I screamed "Enough!" at the top of my lungs. I told myself no more empty promises, and I haven't stopped running since.

When you reach this tipping point, you'll know. Your excuses will make you nauseous. You will feel sick to your stomach because you'll finally realize that you're lying to yourself. That's all an excuse is ... a lie.

Maybe the biggest lie of all is "I'm too busy!"

It's such a blatant lie I stopped using the word "busy" altogether. It's not a busy thing. It's a priority thing. If something is important enough to you, you will find a way to do it – whether that's calling your mom, going on that weekend getaway with your best friend, or rearranging your sock drawer.

We all have a lot going on, but not enough to keep us from logging into Facebook, Instagram, or TikTok. (*The average American spends almost thirty-seven days a year on social media! Thirty-seven days!*)

Instead of saying "I'm too busy," we need to say, "That's not the most important thing in my life right now" or "there are other things more important."

Looking at life from that perspective will get you to the point of *enough,* quickly.

When I started my running streak, I stopped lying to myself.

"Too drunk to run? Whatever. Let's ride!"

Here is that story: I was in New Orleans for business. I worked for an ad agency in Fort Worth, and the Athletics Department at Tulane University was one of my clients. We worked on an outside-the-box marketing campaign that required me to spend weeks at a time in the Big Easy. (*I love New Orleans, so this was an awesome gig.*)

One night, my client took me out on the town.

We ate charbroiled oysters just off Bourbon Street, washing down the buttery and garlicky goodness with cold beers. After that, we went to the iconic Pat O'Brien's — home of the Hurricane. They invented this potent rum drink at Pat O'Brien's. I was told these drinks were legendary and they would put me on my ass.

I drank one Hurricane and started a second when it got to that all-too-familiar part of the night. The moment where all the booze sneaks up on you, taps you on the shoulder, and whispers in your ear, "You better get the hell out of here, bro!"

We did.

I went back to my hotel room and remembered I had not run that day.

"Shit!"

After giving myself a brief pep talk in the bathroom mirror, I put on my shorts and running shoes. I found the hotel gym. The treadmill was oblivious to the magnitude of the situation. My running streak was six months old, definitely in jeopardy, and I was wasted — probably one of my top ten most all-time drunks.

But ... again ... zero excuses!

As I stepped on the treadmill, I kept whispering to myself, "Don't you dare throw up. Don't you dare throw up."

As the treadmill started revving up, I gave myself some last-second words of encouragement. I said out loud, "You don't have to go fast. It's just one mile. Just keep moving. Do *not* throw up!"

I ran 5,280 feet *(one mile)* and not one step further, but I did it. I finished. It might have been the most satisfying run of my life. When you get to the point of *enough,* and you give your excuses the middle finger, it's an empowering reminder that you're in control and that you're unstoppable.

Here is one more poignant example where I had to push through my head trash. This one had to do with running while sick. It was two days after my running streak turned four years old. Running every day was just a part of who I had become.

In a blog post celebrating day number 1,000 of my streak, I wrote:

> *...running every day has become so second nature for me. It's become cemented into my daily thread, and it's not a big deal anymore. Honestly, the only time I'm completely aware of the streak is when I have something out of the ordinary on my To Do List, and I'm forced to shuffle things around and/or plan ahead.*

Two days after my running streak turned four years old, that "out of the ordinary" was a stomach bug. I was convinced it had evolved from some Amazonian region of the planet to devour me from the inside out. To say that I was a sick boy would be a huge understatement.

At one point, I told my mom and my wife to go ahead and start reacquainting themselves with my desired funeral plans. They said I was being over-dramatic and told me to drink more fluids.

I won't disgust you with all the details, but ... *they were gory.*

After the fourth or fifth hour — with no hope in sight — I thought about my running streak. I laid in my bed, whispering to myself, "I still have to run. I still have to run. I still have to run."

Just for the record ... there was never a question of whether I would run. It was simply a matter of when *and* how ugly it was going to be.

After seven hours spent between my bed and my porcelain throne of despair, it was time to *get it on.* "You can do this," I whispered to myself as I put on my running shoes. "It's only one mile."

My head was pounding, and my eyes burned when I closed them.

I was toeing the line of dehydration, and it wasn't going to get any better. I knew that I had to run, and I had to do it right then and there.

I took one last gulp of Gatorade and walked out the front door.

The fresh air was nice, giving me a blast of confidence.

"You can do this...."

I took a deep and intentional breath and ran — *very* slowly. I figured my pace was around twelve or thirteen minutes a mile. I didn't care, though. My goals were to finish *and* not poop on myself.

"It's only one mile!"

I took a lot of deep breaths and would close my eyes for ten to twelve steps at a time as I ran. It reminded me of my third attempt at running a marathon when I pulled myself off the course at Mile 24 and posted an embarrassing DNF *(that's the demoralizing acronym for "Did Not Finish").*

Not long into the run, my weary mind started to wander. For the first time in a while, I thought about my running streak ... while I ran.

I thought about *all* the times I could have just stopped before I went a mile *or* simply not run at all.

*No one would have ever known,* I thought.

I felt a confident smirk reveal itself on my face.

*That's the greatest part of this streak,* I thought as that smirk evolved into a smile. *It's not about anyone else. It's about me!*

*It's about being honest with myself.*

*It's about pushing myself.*

*It's about holding myself accountable.*

I thought back to running all juiced-up in New Orleans. That NOLA run reminded me that the phrase "no one will ever find out" is unacceptable in my world, and the thought of skipping a day or cutting a run short has *never* been an option.

I felt that same way running with that stomach bug — my head pounded and my hiney completely raw. *I could stop right now, and no one would know the difference,* I reminded myself on that sickly run, *but what would be the point?*

I would be lying to everyone, but more importantly … I'd be lying to myself.

"That's what this streak is all about," I whispered. "It's about personal integrity."

With less than a quarter-mile to go, I started to feel extremely weak, but my muscle memory in my legs took over and carried me. I kept it slow and steady — one foot in front of the other.

I threw up a little in my mouth — saltine crackers and orange Gatorade. I swallowed it and kept going.

When I went 5,280 feet *(exactly one mile)*, I stopped. I took one more deep and intentional breath, and that confident smirk revealed itself again.

Then … I waddled back into the house and straight to the bathroom.

# 18

*Lesson 2: Be able to sleep in a storm*
*(Finding contentment).*

Sometimes that fed-upness, the feeling of enough is enough, just never comes. These instances are an indication that you're exactly where you need to be. Maybe not forever, but God has placed, and kept, you there for a reason. When you find yourself in this place, the key is to find contentment without getting too comfortable.

Now, do not let the word "content" or "contentment" confuse you. I did not say "satisfied." There is a huge difference. Contentment is believing — without a doubt in your heart and soul — that you're exactly where you're supposed to be in life. Whether you're flying high — king of your metaphorical mountain — or if you're down on your luck and lying face down in a metaphorical ditch. It's acknowledging that God has a plan, and this is just part of your journey.

It means you're living with no regrets. It means you're not logging into social media and comparing your life through everyone else's filtered images. (*It's called Facebook envy. It's real.*)

Being content means you never play the wildly popular board game, "Woulda, Coulda, Shoulda."

*My life woulda been so much better if I did _____.*
*My life coulda been great if I only had _____.*
*I shoulda done _____ instead of _____.*

That is a dangerous and counterproductive game that ends with you feeling like shit.

Being content with your life means acknowledging and accepting every twist and turn your life has taken. It means recognizing every stupid and reckless decision you've made, and embracing your story — the good, the bad, and the ugly. It is understanding you're right where you are for a reason.

When we find that contentment, that's when we can begin to grow and evolve into the best versions of ourselves.

What can we do? How can we get to the point of contentment? How can we embrace where we are to start to grow and be the best versions of ourselves?

### #1: STOP COMPARING YOURSELF TO OTHER PEOPLE.

For one thing, we have to stop looking over our shoulders at everyone else. We have to stop comparing ourselves to our family members, friends, and neighbors. We have to look inside and remind ourselves we are a one-of-a-kind masterpiece, created by the most amazing "painter" in the history of forever.

You have to remember that there has never been — and there never will be – anyone like you. I have to remember there will always and forever be only one me. Recognizing and celebrating that rarity cuts through the "woe is me" attitude. It gives Facebook envy the middle finger. It gives us peace and moves us closer to contentment.

Spoiler alert: This is not easy, especially if you've been knocked down again and again. If you're in a dark moment of your life, it's not easy to accept you're standing amid the darkness for a reason. It takes patience. It takes faith. It takes courage, self-love, and showing yourself grace.

And, just maybe, it takes trusting someone who's been there before.

## #2: TRUST YOURSELF AND OTHERS

Here is one of my favorite fatherhood stories that exemplifies that.

My son has always loved to make tents.

When he was growing up, if you secured a sheet or blanket to a lamp and then draped it over a random piece of furniture — he was a happy "camper." We built some *monster* tents throughout his childhood — even using the ceiling fan as an anchor point. The more elaborate, the better.

"We might need one more blanket, Daddy."

"Do you think you can put this way up there, Daddy?"

"Our tent needs a sun porch, Daddy."

The funny thing, Crash loved building and playing in these tents, but he didn't want to sleep in them for some reason. He was pretty adamant against it.

I often wondered how he would respond to the chance to sleep in a real tent. Would he do it? Well, that opportunity presented itself when he was four years old.

"Do you want to sleep in daddy's tent outside?" *I asked him.*

Without hesitation, Crash said, "*Yes. Please.*"

He jumped all over it, but I had my doubts.

We pitched a tent on my folks' forty acres. We weren't in the middle of nowhere, but we weren't in the living room anymore, either. I had camped for a couple of days by myself, but I wanted to invite him on the adventure for the last night. I was not sure how this was going to play out.

Before we turned in for the evening, we gathered wood and made a small fire. We did our camp chores. We listened to music and sang *(as a four-year-old, he loved the song God Bless America).* And as dusk faded, we read one of his favorite books by flashlight inside the tent.

Then, it was time to close our eyes and go to sleep. Things were going great, but I had prepared myself for "Let's go back to the house, Daddy!"

I figured he was destined to get to the point of *enough*. It happened every time we made a tent in the house.

This time, it never came.

However, we did play a rousing game of "what if" as the sounds of the night crept into our tent.

"What if a raccoon gets in our tent, Daddy?"

"What if a skunk sprays us through the window, Daddy?"

"What if a bad guy knocks down our tent, Daddy?"

I wouldn't go as far as to say that my four-year-old son was scared, but he was definitely uneasy.

I answered each of his questions with care, but after question forty-three, I simply said, "Crash, I love you more than life itself. You're my boy. I will never let anything happen to you. Plus, God is watching over both of us. There is nothing to be scared of."

"I know, Daddy."

There were no more questions.

The next thing I knew, Crash was snoring like a grown man.

The night was perfect. A slight breeze blew through the tent all night. The temperature was warm — not hot at all for a June night in Texas. The air was faintly sticky.

Just before sunrise, however, a storm blew in. The rain came hard and fast. It was loud. The strong wind rattled the tent.

My son just kept sleeping.

The moment reminded me of a wonderfully great story in Mitch Albom's book, *Have a Little Faith.*

This is an excerpt from a sermon given by Albom's rabbi in 1975, and I thought it was appropriate to share:

> *A man seeks employment on a farm. He hands his letter of recommendation to his new employer. It reads simply, 'He sleeps in a storm.'*
> *The owner is desperate for help, so he hires the man.*
> *Several weeks pass, and suddenly, in the middle of the night, a powerful storm rips through the valley.*

*Awakened by the swirling rain and howling wind, the owner leaps out of bed. He calls for his new hired hand, but the man is sleeping soundly. So he dashes off to the barn. He sees, to his amazement, that the animals are secure with plenty of feed.*

*He runs out to the field. He sees the bales of wheat have been bound and are wrapped in tarps.*

*He races to the silo. The doors are latched, and the grain is dry.*

*And then he understands. 'He sleeps in a storm.'*

This is the part of the sermon I thought about as my son slept soundly, the rain pelting the nylon tent:

*My friends, if we tend to the things that are important in life, if we are right with those we love and behave in line with our faith, our lives will not be cursed with the aching throb of unfulfilled business. Our words will always be sincere, our embraces tight. We will never wallow in the agony of 'I could have, I should have.' We can sleep in a storm.*

A clatter of thunder eventually woke up The Boy.

Again, I was waiting for the "I've had *enough* ... let's go" — but it never came. He simply grabbed the blanket, pulled it up to his chin, and smiled.

"This is so cozy, daddy."

We laid there for thirty to forty-five minutes, just listening to the wind, rain, and thunder.

We were right where we were supposed to be.

Regarding our lives, that realization is powerful. When we trust that we've come prepared and trust the people around us, we're content with where we are. Even if we're in the middle of a "storm."

**#3: DO YOU.**

Since you know my story — how I had eleven jobs in eleven years — the following statement probably won't surprise you. I wasn't content for a long time because I couldn't find the right career path. I took jobs because they matched what my degree said I should do or what my family expected of me. I was in a hurry to find my path.

Then I came across this passage in Matthew Kelly's incredible book, *The Rhythm of Life*. The first time I read it, it gave me peace.

> *The first lesson in finding and following your own star is patience. Many people lose their chance at greatness by chasing after the first star that rises. We should wait and prepare patiently for our star to rise. It will not rise early. It will not rise late. It will rise in the fullness of time—at the most appropriate moment. You need not worry that you will not be ready. It will not rise until you are. You need not fear that you will miss it or fail to recognize it. It is looking for you even more than you are looking for it. It will help you to fulfill the purpose of your existence, and your whole life is leading you toward it.*

Facebook envy, which I mentioned before, can make you roll your eyes when you read Matthew Kelly's words of hope and encouragement. What is Facebook envy? It's a painful feeling you get when you come across your friends on Facebook and begin to think their lives are much more interesting, joyful, and worthwhile than yours. Some scientists — I guess with nothing else to do — determined: "…watching your friends' holidays, love-lives, and business-successes on Facebook can create envy in you. Which can then set off emotions of anguish and loneliness."

Research has showed that one-third of people felt worse and more frustrated with their lives after going onto Facebook. *(I'm sure you can include all the social media platforms in this discussion, too.)* The number one source of animosity, according to these bored scientists, was vacation photos. Holiday pics were a close second.

Another reason for social media envy: comparison of social interaction. The users compared how many birthday greetings they received against their Facebook friends', and they counted how many Likes or remarks they received on their posts.

This is the last thing I will say about Facebook envy, and then we're going to move on. This is important research. According to one survey, eighty percent of people between the ages of eighteen and twenty-nine scroll Facebook while using the restroom. I'm outside that demographic, but I've done it, too. I bet you have too.

Here is the big takeaway: There are millions of people who are frustrated and envious and living under a cloud of anguish or "woe is me" *because* only a handful of their "friends" liked their vacation photos. This, while they were sitting on the toilet taking a shit.

If you need to read that again, please do.

But that's the world that we live in. It's real. I'm not discounting those emotions in any shape, form, or fashion. My problem with Facebook envy is it sets you in a tailspin of trying to keep up with the Joneses, to be like everyone else. It keeps you from being fully yourself, when in truth, the path to *your* contentment is yours alone.

This excerpt from Mitch Albom's rabbi is worth repeating:

> *My friends, if we tend to the things that are important in life, if we are right with those we love and behave in line with our faith, our lives will not be cursed with the aching throb of unfulfilled business. Our words will always be sincere, our embraces tight. We will never wallow in the agony of 'I could have, I should have.' We can sleep in a storm.*

# 19

## Lesson 3: Make the important things important.

Make the important things important. That is a powerful charge. I adopted it in the summer of 2019. I was forty-four years old. Two things happened that made me wrap my arms around that ideal.

The first thing was a solo adventure I took to Big Bend National Park. I had always wanted to go to Big Bend. It was on my first life list. I never did. I *always* had a reason or an excuse not to go.

I remember the judgment from other Texans when I told them. And don't get me started on non-Texans who had spent time in one of the state's ultimate treasures. There was usually an abomination in their judgment.

I judged myself for not doing it, too.

That summer, I said, "No more excuses."

A songwriter friend of mine was hosting a music festival in Marathon, Texas, in late August. Marathon is a lost little town just north of Big Bend. I decided to take a couple of days for myself, explore the National Park, and then spend a couple more in Marathon, enjoying incredible music.

I had it all planned out — except for my two sisters scheduling my mom's seventy-fifth birthday party that same weekend. I had gotten to the point of *enough* regarding my excuses of not going to Big Bend, so I wasn't about to let this stop me. I moved my trip up a couple of days and decided I'd only spend one day at the Marathon Songwriter's Festival. I planned to roll back into town the afternoon of the party. It went off without a hitch. I spent a few days on a solo adventure, listened to great music in a sleepy South Texas town, *and* arrived home in time to celebrate my mom's milestone birthday.

This trip was important.

I hadn't wholeheartedly realized that until I had a conversation with iconic Texas songwriter Walt Wilkins in Marathon. Walt had been on my show a couple of times, and we had become friends. I got three minutes with him after Josh Grider's set and before Drew Kennedy took the stage. *(If you don't know who these artists are, look them up on Spotify. You're welcome in advance.)*

I told Walt about my solo adventure. About getting to the place of *enough* and refusing to make any more excuses. I shared with him my trip to that point and how I bagged Emory Peak, the highest point in the park. I told him that I tent-camped and got invaded by fire ants in the middle of the night. I told him how I had to strip down in the middle of a hike and slipped into Langford Hot Springs on the banks of the Rio Grande River, a stone's throw from Mexico. I also told him that I was leaving that night to be back in Rainbow for my mom's party.

Walt looked me in the eye and said — like only Walt Wilkins can say, "I'm glad you did that because that's important."

It was the way he said "important" that stuck with me. He was right. It was important for me to pack up the truck and drive almost 1,000 miles round-trip to go on this adventure finally. It was vital for me to do it by myself. It was essential to adjust on the move when my sisters told me the date of my mom's party. It was important that I didn't create another bullshit excuse and say, "I'll do it next summer."

It took the perspective of a legendary songwriter on the Texas Music scene to open my eyes. If you know Walt Wilkins, you know it wasn't just the way he said it; it was the look in his eye when he told me, "I'm glad you did that, because that's important."

Standing there in the dry Marathon heat, I was grateful for that perspective. Walt Wilkins had planted a powerful seed deep inside my soul.

Almost three weeks later, a horrific tragedy watered that seed with a deafening "life is short" whisper — those reminders from God that life is short ... life is precious ... and we better start acting accordingly.

I received the message mid-morning on September 5, 2019. I had just finished recording my radio show and podcast in Fort Worth. It was a simple message, "Sorry to hear about Kylie Rae. So sad."

Kylie Rae Harris had come on my live-audience radio show earlier that year. Before that show, Kylie and I were acquaintances. But because of the nature of my shows, I get to know my guests pretty well. Even sitting in front of 85 to 100 people, it's a very intimate experience listening to them share their stories, asking questions about who they are and what matters most to them. At these particular shows — which showcased singer/songwriters on the Texas Music scene — they would play several songs for me throughout our two-hour conversation. There is a definite connection.

After my live audience show on March 31, 2019, I felt I knew Kylie Rae Harris. I considered her a friend.

On Sept. 5 of that same year — a mere five months after that live-audience show — Kylie Rae Harris died in a two-car accident outside Taos, New Mexico. A sixteen-year-old girl from the area was killed, too. I won't get into all the details of the crash because it doesn't matter for this book. It was tragic for everyone involved. Two people died.

Kylie Rae Harris and I weren't best friends. Many others knew and loved her on a much deeper level. But her sudden death rocked my world.

After briefly searching social media and news reports, I confirmed she was gone.

I remember sitting in my truck and crying.

I thought about her daughter, Corbie, and cried more.

During my live-audience show, Kylie sang *Twenty Years*, which she had written for Corbie. At the time of the show, Corbie was six years old. She tagged along with her mom that particular day. Corbie was at the show.

After Kylie set up the song, I asked her if I could bring Corbie on stage while she sang. She passed the buck to Corbie, thinking her daughter wouldn't sit in front of a theatre full of people. But she did.

As Kylie started to sing, she looked out into the darkness of the theatre, the stage lights blinding her from the anticipation in the audience. She had a lump in her throat. "Drew, I don't know if I can do this."

I gave her a vote of confidence through my wireless mic and the house speakers. I stood in the darkness, waiting with as much anticipation as everyone else.

She was able to sing it, and it was powerful.

As I sat in my truck and cried after hearing about her death, I thought about that moment on stage at that small theatre in Granbury, Texas. The chorus from the song haunted me. It haunted all of us — anyone and everyone who considered Kylie Rae Harris a friend.

> *Twenty years from now*
> *My prayer is that somehow*
> *You'll forgive all my mistakes*
> *And be proud of the choice I make*
> *God, I hope I'm still around*
> *Twenty years from now*

As the days passed and the horrible details of Kylie's accident came out, I just kept asking myself, "I hope she made the important things important in her life?"

When I brought these singer/songwriters on my show, I asked each of them if they had a life list or a bucket list. It was a good conversation starter wrapped around their goals, dreams, and aspirations. Some artists did. Most didn't have a written list. We'd brainstorm ideas. Then, they would play another song.

After Kylie died, I didn't think about her life list. It wasn't about playing a show at the legendary Red Rocks Amphitheatre outside of Denver. It wasn't about smoking a joint with Willie Nelson on his tour bus *(which Kylie Rae had possibly done)*. It wasn't about going skydiving, or summiting Mt. Everest, or throwing out the first pitch at a Major League Baseball game.

For several weeks after her death, I wondered if she had made the important things important. Did Corbie know how much her mom loved her? Did her friends know how much she cherished them? Did her mom know that she was her rock?

*Make the important things important.*

*Make the important things important.*

*Make the important things important.*

I couldn't stop saying those words. Over and over and over again.

Then, I flipped the narrative and put my life in the crosshairs. "Am I making the important things important?"

I asked myself the million-dollar questions, "What is important to me?"

What I quickly started to love about this charge of "make the important things important" ... I realized how personal it was. I recognized that what's important to me is different from what's important to you. Each of us has to decide what's important to us and then emphasize *that*.

I can't tell you in *Tacos and Chocolate* what should be important in your life. That realization falls directly on your shoulders.

I can provide some guidance, though.

Let's play a game. Close your eyes for thirty seconds, and quickly make a mental list of important things in your life.

Go ahead. I'll wait.

Here's the game: Even though I can't tell you what needs to be important in your life, I can make some assumptions about what's on your mental list *(or not on your list)*.

You probably listed time, relationships, and purpose. If you stayed practical, you probably put food, water, and sleep on your list of important things in your life.

I'm going to step out on a limb and assume that social media or TV were *not* on your list of the important things in your life. Is that a safe assumption? You didn't list HGTV or reruns of *Friends*, right? Your Facebook timeline didn't make the list either, correct?

I'm assuming your answer is no.

Thank goodness.

But here is some radical honesty: Statistics show that social media and TV — any and all screen time — are extremely important to us. Here are some fun facts *(and when I say "fun," I mean entirely embarrassing and disgusting):*

- The average American spends almost two and a half hours a day on social media. That equates to 876 hours a year. For all of those non-math majors, that breaks down to thirty-seven days a year. *(See ... I wasn't lying two chapters ago!)* The average American spends more than one month a year looking to see if their high school friends got fat on Facebook or sharing photos of their lunch on Instagram.

- The average American watches three and a half hours of TV every day. That equates to 1,260 hours a year or fifty-two days. That is a lot of *CSI: Miami, Love It or List It,* and *Monday Night Football.*

So here's my question: If social media and TV are *not* on our list of the important things in our lives, why do they account for 121 days out of the year? Why are we spending four months a year in front of a screen? That is a third of the calendar year engaged in something that allegedly is not important to us.

For a frame of reference, here is an interesting statistic from the U.S. Department of Health and Human Services: Less than 5 percent of adults participate in 30 minutes of physical activity each day; only one in three adults receive the recommended amount of physical activity each week.

Here is another one. This stat is from Pew Research Center: About 25 percent of American adults said they haven't read a book in the last year in any form.

So that sparks another pressing question ... Are we making ourselves important? Are we emphasizing our mental, physical, emotional, and spiritual wellbeing? According to some of the research, we're not.

According to one Harris Poll, only one-third of Americans claim to be happy. An even more tragic number: Only 67 percent of the 2,345 respondents in the same poll were optimistic about the future. The rest had no hope for a better tomorrow.

I firmly believe the bleak outlook has everything to do with not putting ourselves on our list of the important things. We become an afterthought. We give ourselves the scraps after pouring our energy into our kids, our jobs, our social media addiction. In the next couple of chapters, I'm going to share the part of my story where I was living that way — where I lost sight of putting an emphasis on myself and loving me.

After my conversation with Walt Walkins, and the tragic death of Kylie Rae Harris, I encouraged others to make the important things important, but I was leaving out a significant part to that charge. I missed the most crucial piece of the puzzle.

I stopped *just* telling people to "make the important things important" and added three essential words, "Starting with *you.*"

# 20

## Lesson 4: Ask yourself, "What's next?"

If you haven't read *The Miracle Morning* by Hal Elrod, I encourage you to do so. It's a solid read, and his charge to win your mornings is inspiring. I'll go ahead and be bold – it's a game-changer. It helped change my life.

If you love *Tacos and Chocolate,* and you don't want to stop and read Hal's book right now, here is a million-mile overview: When we feed our souls every morning, we lay a solid foundation for the rest of the day. Hal Elrod put together a game plan for how to accomplish that goal. He used the acronym "SAVERS" to make it stick. His morning routine consisted of silence, affirmations, visualization, exercise, reading, and scribing.

I thought it was fantastic. I bought into the life-changing recipe Elrod was cookin' up.

After reading his book, I woke up every day and did five of those six things. I meditated and prayed *(silence)*. I stared at my vision board *(visualization)*. I worked out and ran *(exercise)*. I read, and I did free writing exercises in my journal *(scribing)*. *(I didn't embrace the affirmations. More on that in a minute.)*

I'm not going to sugarcoat this; it was effing awesome. After I went through Hal's morning routine, I was on fire. I realized the importance of attacking the day, focusing on myself, and refusing to let "life" — kids, work, bills, social media — drive the narrative. It was about being in control of my mental, emotional, physical, and spiritual wellbeing.

The trouble was, my current routine wasn't sustainable. I was spending almost two hours every day on these miraculous mornings. If I didn't get my reading done, or I mailed it in during my meditation, I felt guilty. Then, the stress crept in. This beautiful and powerful game plan was beginning to backfire. So, I did what most people would do — yes, I fell in line with the masses and temporarily became a card-carrying member of the status quo — I just stopped winning my morning. There was no more reading, prayer, meditation, or working out. I was done. It might be over-the-top dramatic to say that I quit, but I did.

For about eighteen months, my mornings became very reactionary. I was no longer attacking the day or driving the narrative. I was not laying the foundation for any personal growth and development. By not winning my mornings, I went through my days in a fog. I was going through the motions. Treading water. Burning up that hamster wheel. I was still in the fight, but just barely. I wasn't kicking any ass.

In the fall of 2019, I started to slide. I was lost. I didn't know which way was up. I found myself in a very dark and isolated place.

The day before Thanksgiving in 2019, I hit rock bottom. My wife had taken the kids to her parents' house. I wasn't invited. My marriage was in a bad place, and I was on the verge of spending Thanksgiving alone. I was sober at this point, but all I wanted to do that night was play "How Drunk Can I Get?"

It's not a fun game when you're all alone. It's destructive. I played it on my 25th birthday as well, finishing a bottle of cheap chardonnay all by myself in my Wichita Falls apartment. I crushed it, finishing the cut-rate wine in less than an hour. I think I was disqualified from the game after spending my milestone birthday on the cold bathroom floor — that's *after* calling a friend and proclaiming my love. (*shout out to Julie Duncan.*)

So, on Thanksgiving Eve of 2019, I stood alone in front of our garage refrigerator. With the cold concrete floor beneath my feet, I stared at my wife's beer in the fridge. I stared at it for a long time. I wanted to drink so much that I ended up on the bathroom floor again. I wanted to violently throw up — a vomit where the tears and snot just flow out, too.

My thought process: It will feel better than what I'm feeling right now.

I didn't drink that night. Unless you count delicious Mexican mineral water. I grabbed a Topo Chico out of the refrigerator instead of a Corona or Shiner Bock.

That was a win.

Later that evening, when I stood in the kitchen and stared at the butcher knife on the counter for five minutes, I knew I had to make a change. I'm not saying I would do anything with that knife, but I stood there for five minutes, eyes locked on it. I can't remember what was going through my head, but it couldn't have been good.

Real quick: About suicide, it's not in my nature to kill myself. I've said this many times. I'm too big of a pussy to take my own life. That particular night, I think I just wanted to hurt myself. I wanted to feel something different.

I didn't harm myself. Just like the beer in the refrigerator, I eventually broke my stare and walked away from the knife.

The rest of that night was a blur. I think I made a fire in the fireplace and watched a movie. I know that I slept on the couch, and I remember making a vital decision before falling asleep.

My sister, Susan, and her family do a "homemade" Turkey Trot around their Dallas neighborhood on Thanksgiving morning. They make running bibs, and they map out a course. They invite neighbors and friends over. It's organic and fun. Some people run. A lot of people walk. Some of the kids ride their bikes through the tree-lined streets of the posh part of Dallas.

I had never participated. I always had a hundred excuses why I couldn't go. The main one was I didn't want to.

But before I went to bed that night, I received a whisper from God. He said, "Go."

Now, I need to clear something up really quick for those who don't have strong faith. I did *not* hear an audible voice telling me to participate in a makeshift 5K in Dallas, Texas. That is why I say it was a "whisper."

As I laid on the couch watching a movie, I was inspired to take action. To move. To not sit still and wallow in my anger, sadness, and confusion. That thought and inspiration came from somewhere. In my world, that is God talking to me. That is the Holy Spirit moving me.

The following day, I woke up around 5:30 am. It was cold and wet outside. I sent my sister a text message.

Me: *Is your Turkey Trot rain or shine? Asking for a friend before he drives in from Rainbow, Texas.*

She said the rain had slowed down.

Susan: *I think we're going for it. Yay! I didn't know you were coming. Bundle up!*

Eight hours before that text, I didn't know I was going either. There was something powerful about making that hard decision to go — despite the hour and a half drive ... despite the cold and rain ... despite the fact I locked eyes with a butcher knife for five minutes earlier that night.

The intentionality about deciding to "go" was the powerful part.

Because of that text, Susan was the only person who knew my plans. My wife didn't know. My parents, who had invited me to spend Thanksgiving at their house, didn't know. I had made an executive decision for myself. That is what I needed to do at that moment. I was in control.

When I left Rainbow, it was dark. It was cold. It was wet. But for the first time in several months, I didn't feel numb. I was excited about doing this homespun holiday 5K. Even though I was making a drive that I had made hundreds of times, it felt like I was on an ultimate Thanksgiving adventure. *(Ultimate might be a little strong, but an adventure nonetheless.)*

Looking back, I realize that is what my soul needed.

The "Oak Cliff Turkey Trot" was fun. We started at my sister's house and ran through the streets of her neighborhood, stopping at her friends' houses for water, mimosas, and hot chocolate. Our last stop was at a funky, cool loft in Bishop Arts. We ate brunch together, and I was humbly reminded of how rich people live.

Afterward, both my sisters asked me to stay and spend Thanksgiving with them. They knew I was in a weird place, and they knew my wife and kids were spending Thanksgiving 220 miles away from me.

My sisters didn't beg me to stay — they just asked a couple of times nicely. I politely declined. I wanted the adventure to continue. I wasn't sure what was coming next, but that's what excited me.

As I pulled out of Susan's driveway, I whispered to myself, "Now what? What's next?"

It's kind of strange, but I thought back to that hut-to-hut bike ride I did in Colorado back in 2002. On that trip, I rode almost 100 miles on a mountain bike through the western part of the state. As I pedaled my mountain bike up 3,000 feet over a twelve-mile stretch — legs and lungs yearning for a quiet vacation on a tropical beach — I wrestled with my definition of "adventure."

I thought about that story on my way back to Rainbow, Texas, on that Thanksgiving morning.

Before that ride through the western slope of the Rocky Mountains, I struggled with that definition. I couldn't verbalize what "going on an adventure" really meant. When I was screaming down the backside of the mountain — dropping 3,000 feet in five miles on two wheels — I started to get a pretty good grasp of that elusive explanation.

This is what I came up with on that epic trip (*make sure you read the entire blog post at the back of the book*): When you aren't 100 percent sure what's coming around the next corner, whether that's on the side of a mountain or walking down an unfamiliar street, you are in the midst of an adventure.

I was definitely in the midst of an adventure on that Thanksgiving — mentally, emotionally, and spiritually.

– – –

"What's next?"

After the Turkey Trot, I decided to work a little. Weird? Not for a guy who loves to work, which I do.

I found an open Starbucks, and I set up shop editing my radio show and podcast. At that time, I had a daily show on Real Texas Radio and True Texas Radio, two internet radio stations in the region. This was another big win because I seriously thought about *not* releasing a show that week. It was scheduled to run that day on Real Texas Radio and the next day on True Texas Radio. No one would have noticed or thought anything about it, but I wanted to get it out. It was important to me for some reason. I think it had to do with being in control of something. Anything.

After editing, producing, and uploading a radio show that probably *zero* people listened to, I was starving, and there was no turkey and dressing for miles. I was convinced there would be a Chinese food restaurant slinging egg rolls on Thanksgiving. I was wrong. I did find an Olive Garden that was open, but I just couldn't pull the trigger. "All you can eat breadsticks" is the devil for someone who lives a gluten-conscious lifestyle.

I headed south on Hwy 67 with my eyes open and stomach growling. I passed through one town. Then another. Then another. Nothing was open. I get it. Ordinary people were sitting around a big table with family members they don't really know, asking them to pass the candied yams. *(I don't know why I said that. We never passed our Thanksgiving feasts. It was always buffet-style. In the same breath ... no one ever carved the turkey at the end of the table — someone stood in the corner of the kitchen and picked the meat off with their fingers. Sometimes, I wish I lived in the movies.)*

I digress.

No food. Really hungry. Alone.

Loving every second of it.

When I was twenty minutes from the house, I got off the highway and drove down a main street in Cleburne, Texas *(shout out to everyone who lives in southern Johnson County)*. Even though the holiday cards were stacked against me, I was optimistic. My mind was consumed with combination fried rice and orange chicken, but then it happened. I saw the flashing "OPEN" sign on the side of a neon green taco truck. It was shining like a beacon of freedom. *Screw those egg rolls.*

Besides, the title of this book is *The Tacos and Chocolate Diet; The Egg Rolls and Chocolate Diet* doesn't exactly roll off the tongue.

I pulled into the parking lot of an abandoned hair salon, where the neon green taco truck was parked and walked up to the window. The "Cash Only" sign didn't even phase me. I had eight $1 bills in my pocket and a bottle of water in the truck. I was about to eat like a Thanksgiving king.

I ordered four bean and pico de gallo tacos on corn tortillas to honor my gluten-conscious and plant-based diet. *(FYI: Even if I did stumble upon the mythical Chinese restaurant that was allegedly open on Thanksgiving, I couldn't have eaten an egg roll because of my diet.)*

I sat in my truck, eating some of the best tacos I've ever put in my mouth, listening to the Cowboys game on the radio. I was alone on Thanksgiving. No one was looking for me. And I was entirely at peace.

My soul wasn't aching. I didn't feel lost. I didn't have angst raging inside me. At that point, I realized I had started the healing process.

I had rediscovered hope by simply asking myself, "What's Next?"

# 21

*Lesson 5: Focus on a single win*
*(#myonething).*

That's not the end of my Thanksgiving tale.
Of course, I didn't know it at the time, but Thanksgiving Day in 2019 was a springboard to a new life for me.

As I ate my delicious tacos, I reflected on the past twenty-four hours.

It seemed so rudimentary – almost silly – to say, but the following series of events pulled me out of a dark rut:

- ○ A folksy neighborhood Turkey Trot;
- ○ Producing a radio show/podcast that no one was going to listen to, and
- ○ Eating vegan tacos on corn tortillas from a neon green food truck in Cleburne, Texas.

Let me clarify. It wasn't those actual events that changed my trajectory. It was the decision not to sit still and let the darkness continue to crush my soul. It was the choice to listen to God's whisper and move. Take action. Make executive decisions – even though they were so simple.

I think so many people sit still and let the wave of darkness overtake them. Whether you're talking about TVs, phones, or tablets, I think screens have left us paralyzed and susceptible to that darkness.

Author Mel Robbins has a powerful way to get your butt moving. It's called the *5 Second Rule*, and it's simple and genius. On her blog, she broke it down:

> *There is a window that exists between the moment you have an instinct to change and your mind killing it. It's a 5 second window. And it exists for everyone. If you do not take action on your instinct to change, you will stay stagnant. You will not change.*

To execute the *5 Second Rule*, you count down: 5-4-3-2-1. Robbins wrote: "The counting will focus you on the goal or commitment and distract you from the worries, thoughts, and excuses in your mind. As soon as you reach 1 — push yourself to move."

It is so simple, but a powerful way to get your butt moving.

Now, I can't swear that I utilized *The 5 Second Rule* on that infamous Thanksgiving morning, but there *was* a force that made me take action. Something helped me push through my bullshit and head trash so that I would drive to Dallas in the cold rain and run in a 5k cobbled together by my sister.

Was it Mel Robbins? Was it God? Despite the awesomeness of Mel Robbins, it probably was the latter.

This leads me back to Hal Elrod's *Miracle Morning*. (*I know, some of you linear thinkers were starting to worry and lose your shit.*)

I guess this is the million-dollar question: Was my pre-Thanksgiving gloom and murkiness caused by me unintentionally giving Hal Elrod the middle finger and abandoning his proven recipe to transform my life?

I can answer that question with pure confidence: Kind of?

I do know this, without a doubt in my mind ... I had lost sight of my mental, emotional, physical, and spiritual well-being. I stood firmly in the middle of my biggest nightmare; I became like everyone else. The status quo had engulfed me, and my soul was suffocating.

Then, I was thrown a life jacket.

At this point in my story, let me proudly introduce you to my cousin, Mary.

For forty-two years of my life, I didn't know how Mary was related to me. She was one of *those* relatives. I knew she was family, but I had no clue where she fell on our family tree. Not that it matters to this story, but Mary's mom and my mom were first cousins, which made Mary and my mom second cousins.

I don't think third cousin is a thing. I think that is when you start throwing around confusing genealogical phrases like "once removed." So, I just call Mary my cousin.

After Mary's husband passed away, she bought the twelve acres next to us in Rainbow. Mary became more than a second cousin once removed. She became a friend. We started having coffee talks from time to time. I gave her permission to peek behind my curtain. Mainly because I trusted her.

I thoroughly enjoyed those morning conversations. I was getting therapy without a co-pay. Mary is an ordained minister in the Episcopal Church and provides pastoral care for other priests and ministers. She unintentionally became my spiritual mentor. She probably thought we were just catching up over a cup of coffee from time to time, but I was seriously thinking about leaving that copay on her kitchen table after we talked.

She doesn't know this, but she saved my life.

One morning over coffee — a few weeks after my Thanksgiving epiphany — she simply and matter-of-factly said, "Focus on you. Take care of you."

Mary encouraged me to focus on my emotional and mental well-being. She wanted me to turn up the knob on my physical health, primarily regarding sleep. She wanted me to focus on my relationship with God and to grow spiritually.

So I did.

I started by crawling back to Hal Elrod and his concept of *The Miracle Morning*. My tail was officially between my legs, and I was gnawing on a hefty serving of crow. I recognized the previous impact his philosophy had on my mornings and my life. Every part of SAVERS (*Silence, Affirmations, Visualization, Exercise, Reading, and Scribing*) were tools that supported Mary's call to action. Each one of Hal Elrod's habits had the potential to positively impact my physical, mental, emotional and spiritual well-being.

"Let's ride, Hal Elrod! Let's be miraculous!"

5-4-3-2-1... GO!

But I couldn't get started.

I wanted to jump out of bed and do those six things, but instead, I dealt with serious head trash. So, I didn't do anything. I threw around the worst phrase in the English language, "I'll just start tomorrow."

I had followed his game plan before, and it was awesome, but I stopped because it took up anywhere from ninety minutes to two hours every morning.

Here was my head trash: If I started my *Miracle Morning* and didn't finish those five to six things, I felt guilty. If I stayed the course and completed my *Miracle Morning*, I felt guilty that it took so long and cut into my work day. The last thing I wanted to feel as I clawed and scratched and fought my way out of my dark pit was guilt.

That is when #myonething was born. I realized I didn't have to complete all six of Hal's morning tasks to lay a solid foundation for the rest of the day. I only needed one. So, before I went to bed every night, I picked the one thing would do the following day. Maybe it was prayer. Perhaps it was free writing in my journal. Maybe it was exercise. And no matter what, I would do that one thing before anything and everything else.

Earlier in the book, I referenced Admiral William H. McRaven and his book, *Make Your Bed*. It's a solid book, but I need to poke holes in his overarching theme.

When he gave his commencement speech at the University of Texas, he said:

*If you make your bed every morning, you will have accomplished the first task of the day. It will give you a small sense of pride and it will encourage you to do another task and another and another. By the end of the day, that one task completed will have turned into many tasks completed. Making your bed will also reinforce the face that little things in life matter. If you can't do the little things right, you will never do the big things right.*

Admiral McRaven is not wrong. I love all of that — and it's one of ten lessons he learned being a Navy Seal. I refuse to discount anything from his legendary commencement speech or his wildly popular book.

But...

If you're going to accomplish one thing every morning, why wouldn't that one thing be something that fed your soul? Shouldn't it lay a solid foundation for the rest of your day? If you want to make your bed, by all means ... make your bed. But don't let that be your one thing. Make your bed and then pray. Make your bed and then workout or meditate. Make your bed, and then focus on your vision board.

Drinking coffee is in the same family as making your bed. When I'm talking to others about #myonething and how they start their day, a common response is, "The first thing that I do every day is drink coffee."

I get it. I like coffee. It helps wake me up.

Just like making your bed ... drink your coffee, but don't let that be your one thing. That might help get your brain firing, but it's not going to help you get back to center when life starts throwing darts at you.

Drink your coffee; then read a chapter in a book. Drink your coffee; then free-write for fifteen minutes. Drink your coffee; then go for a run. There are a lot of things you could do while you're drinking your coffee or even while it's brewing.

I have a dear friend who challenged me on coffee being her one thing.

Joy said, "I drink coffee before I even go to the bathroom, brush my teeth, or let the dogs out."

"What do you do while your coffee is brewing?" I asked.

"During those ninety seconds?"

"Yes."

"Stare at the Keurig and wipe the sleep from my eyes."

"What if you prayed for those ninety seconds? What if you thanked God for all the blessings in your life or asked him to watch over and protect your boys that day? What if you asked for strength? Guidance? Wisdom?" I said.

"Then what?" she asked.

"Drink your coffee."

– – –

So every day, I'm intentional about choosing to do just one thing that feeds my soul. That could be one of the following things (*Reminder: Your soul-feeding activities could be totally different*):

- Pray
- Affirmations
- Read
- Meditate
- Visualize (using my vision board)
- Workout/run
- Journal

And like I mentioned before, I do *one* of these things without any excuses.

But this might be the most powerful part of #myonething:

That one thing usually turns into two, three, or sometimes five things.

It's a win if I do #myonething, but it's like a juicy cherry on top of a delicious sundae if I can feed my soul with something else.

I'll share an example.

It's a random Tuesday in April. I decide #myonething that particular morning is journaling. No matter what else happens *(kids, dogs, broken water pipes, etc.)*, I'll grab my journal and do ten to fifteen minutes of freewriting. I'm over-the-top intentional about getting this done. No matter what. Zero excuses.

After I scribble in my journal, I can attack the day. I've accomplished #myonething. *But* if there are no broken water pipes, and I have a few more minutes before life starts barreling down the tracks, I might go through my prayer list, too. If I have a little more time, I might go through my vision board.

Boom! Cherry on the top!

#Myonething has the potential to turn into a handful of other things that feed my soul. It helps lay that foundation for the rest of your day. That one thing — whatever you choose — will carry you through the course of your day, but a handful of things that feed your soul will catapult you.

After you get done with your morning routine — when you complete #myonething — I have one more favor to ask: Choose to be happy. Be intentional about making that decision. Start your day in a positive space with your heart full.

Here's why.

Because everything that happens after that moment is a reaction to everything that happens through your day — good, bad, or ugly. When life starts coming at you, you can get back to the center. You can lean on that one thing that fed your soul earlier in the day, and you can remind yourself that you chose to be happy.

# 22

*Lesson 6: Count your wins.*

I've had a good life. It's not even a stretch to say that it has been great. As I'm writing this book, I have some head trash about that. *(I know ... weird to say, but true.)* Aside from the sexual abuse I mentioned early on in the book, nothing horrible has happened to me.

There were no welfare checks or food stamps while growing up. My mom tells a story about making bologna quiche once, but there was always food on the table.

We had nice clothes to wear.

Like I mentioned before, my dad was around. We didn't play catch in the backyard or go on father-son adventures, but he was always there.

There was love in the house.

We never went without.

Overall, it has been a wonderfully great life.

This realization hit me while I was writing this book. I had a conversation with myself. "Nothing bad has happened to me. I've never been forced to overcome adversity. I've never been forced to pull myself out of the muck and grime. I've never been the underdog. Why in the hell would anyone want to read this book, laden with white privilege and blessings?"

I worked through that head trash by reminding myself you and I aren't that different.

If you're reading this, you have *so much* to be grateful for. Is that a bold assumption? Well, there isn't a doubt in my mind ... your blessings are plentiful. You might be going through some dark times. You might be in a rut. But, all in all, your life is pretty effing awesome.

Let me make a handful of assumptions.

Assumption No. 1: You likely woke up with a roof over your head this morning.

Assumption No. 2: You probably have clothes in your closet. *(There is also a great chance that 50 percent of those clothes are clean and smell like Bounce fabric softener.)*

Assumption No. 3: You likely have food in your refrigerator or pantry. *(If you don't ... the cheerful drive-thru worker at McDonald's or Taco Bell knows you by your first name. My point: You're not starving.)*

Assumption No. 4: There is at least one person in this world who loves and cares about you. *(Maybe it's just your mom or your kiddo, but there is someone who would be sad if you vanished into thin air.)*

I could keep going, but hopefully, you get it — hopefully, you understand.

If you're having a pity party today, and you're not interested in buying a cup of the Kool-Aid that I'm serving ... think about this:

- On average, half a million people in the United States sleep on the streets or in homeless shelters every night.
- About 690 million people worldwide go to bed hungry each night.
- In the United States, there are 400,000 children in the foster care system.
- Two-fifths of all older people *(about 3.9 million)* say the television is their main company.

Maybe you fall into one of these statistical categories, but again, if you're reading this book, I bet you don't. (*Hell, 32 million Americans can't read. You should be grateful for that!*)

We're all blessed. We all have so much to be thankful for, but for some reason, we have forgotten how blessed we are. We get lost in the unimportant. We focus on the negative. We compare ourselves to our friends' filtered lives as presented on social media. We constantly want bigger and better and more. We beat ourselves up over trivial "losses" and don't show ourselves grace for being flawed humans.

Some of you are saying, "You don't know me. You don't know what I'm going through."

You're right. I don't. We all have our stuff. Life is not perfect. It's hard sometimes. Bad shit does happen.

But when bad things happen, I have a challenge for you: when you find your thoughts spiraling toward the negative, count your wins, no matter how small. Even when things are good, count your wins. (*It's a good habit you can build when you're up and fall back on when you're down*).

Here's what you do: grab a sheet of paper and a pen and make tally marks all day when something good happens to you. Do it for twenty-four hours.

You weren't stopped by the train this morning on your drive to work ... win ... mark it down. Your kids woke up healthy and were able to go to school and learn ... win and win. (*They did it without a complete meltdown ... another win.*) Your favorite t-shirt was clean ... that's a big win, at least for me. You had enough milk for your cereal and weren't tempted to use water.

I've given people this challenge before – whether I spoke to a community group or teaching a continuing education class at a college or university. Many people struggle with this because they only focus on the "big wins," (*e.g. Today, I got a raise or my girlfriend finally decided to move in with me, or my kids didn't call me an asshole as they were getting ready for school.*)

It's the little wins that make life worth living.

Did you know that an average of 150,000 people die each day? Just waking up is a win. More than 1.8 million people will be diagnosed with cancer this year. If you're healthy ... win! I could keep going — but surely I don't have to.

Regardless, count your wins today. It's a powerful reminder to look at those tallies at the end of the day. It's a gentle whisper that life isn't all doom and gloom. It changes your perspective.

The next step is to celebrate those wins. I'm not saying throw a party when you hit every green light on your way to work, but more often than not, we glance right over these wins. We don't give them the attention and recognition they deserve. Even the big wins.

We downplay them with defeating phrases like:

- "I just got lucky this time."
- "Yeah, but..."
- "I did alright, I guess."

Resilience coach Shawn Ellis shared three reasons why it's important to celebrate the little victories. On his blog, he wrote:

- It makes you feel happy
- It gives you motivation to keep going
- It builds your confidence

Unfortunately, I notice many people don't do this. Even if it's a big win, the recognition and celebration are usually fleeting. I'm guilty of this to a certain degree. I don't want to lose that momentum, so I quickly focus on: "What's next?" (*Hell, I dedicated a whole chapter to that.*)

On the flip side, if we suffer a loss or a setback, we beat the shit out of ourselves. We'll hold on to a loss for hours, sometimes days.

I can't even begin to figure out why we do this, but I think it comes from a place of self-worth. So many don't feel like they deserve to be successful. They don't feel powerful. They don't feel strong. They don't feel like a masterpiece.

I shared this in Chapter 1, but it's worth repeating. It's hard to consider yourself a masterpiece after life has beaten you down.

This is from Og Mandino's narrative *Memorandum from God*. He writes:

> *For how could you be a miracle when you consider yourself a failure at the most menial of tasks? How can you be a miracle when you have little confidence in dealing with the most trivial of responsibilities? How can you be a miracle when you are shackled by debt...*

That is why recognizing and celebrating our wins — even the little ones — is so important. We have started to believe the lie that we're not one-of-a-kind special. That's bullshit. We are. You are. I am.

We have to combat the lie, and that is super simple to do.

Grab a sheet of paper. It can be a paper towel, a piece of junk mail, or a Post It Note – just something to write on. Grab a pen, too. For the next twenty-four hours, count your wins. It could be the most trivial thing ever, like clearing twenty emails out of your Inbox or logging out of social media for an hour.

Let all of those wins generate momentum and feed your confidence.

Then, when you have a big win, I challenge you to be intentional about celebrating that victory. Here are a few ways you can do that:

### *SHOUT IT FROM THE ROOFTOPS (tell someone).*

Don't treat a major accomplishment like a dirty little secret. If you did something badass, let people know – send a text, pick up the phone, call a friend or put it out there on social media.

When I hit the ten-year mark of my running streak, I did a video and posted it on Facebook. I was proud of myself. I told my family and friends I had run at least one mile for the past 3,654 days. Was I bragging? You bet your ass I was.

I hesitated for a hot minute before I reminded myself to "walk the walk." I smirked as my video uploaded. As I waited for it to finish, I saw braggadocious posts about what people ate for lunch, their new haircut, and how many points their kiddo scored in a fourth-grade basketball game.

*TALK TO YOURSELF (repeat your mantra).*

Again, my personal mantra is "Eyes on God ... others first ... no excuses ... I am a warrior — stay in the fight." I love that mantra whether I win *or* lose. It keeps me grounded while giving me a boost of confidence at the same time. If I'm down, it gives me a boost. If I have a big win, it keeps me humble, reminding me who deserves the credit for that accomplishment. We're already talking to ourselves. Why don't we speak to ourselves in an empowering way? I drive this point home in Lesson 7 *(it deserves its own chapter)*.

*GIVE YOURSELF A BREAK (take a rest day).*

I struggle with this because I want to build on that momentum. So, I push. I'm afraid if I rest, I'll lose that velocity. But there is something powerful about taking an intentional break — even if it's a short one. It allows us to reflect, recharge, and get re-focused so we can summit our next mountaintop.

*SAY THANK YOU (take a gratitude pause).*

This might be the most powerful thing you can do when you have a big win. It takes the focus off you and your accomplishment and simply puts the opportunity to be successful in the spotlight. For some, this is going to look a lot like a prayer. That's the case in my world. When I express gratitude for a chance to strive, I'm talking to God.

- - -

All of this is generating momentum and shining a beautiful light on our lives. The powerful quote from Dr. Martin Luther King is the absolute truth: "Darkness cannot drive out darkness, only light can do that. Hate cannot drive out hate, only love can do that."

Where is your focus? What is commanding your attention? Are you recognizing and celebrating your wins or letting the losses define you?

In the tremendous book *The Noticer Returns*, author Andy Andrews wrote:

> *Darkness commands an inordinate amount of attention from a person who is unprepared and unprotected. Attention to darkness produces doubt. When a person is distracted and weakened by struggles, doubt whispers a message logically urging surrender; and soon, that person's focus is on his own discomfort, his fear and anger, regret and resentment.*

That is why counting our wins is so crucial. When we become increasingly aware of our victories — almost expecting them — we start to ignore the losses, or at least minimize the impact they have on our lives.

Then we realize that failure is not fatal. We understand that if we stumble and fall, all we have to do is stand back up. We gain confidence. We start to take risks. We start living boldly, adventurously, and intentionally.

# 23

*Lesson 7: Pay attention to how you talk to yourself.*

L et's discuss how we talk to ourselves.
       You talk to yourself, right?

Spoiler alert: You do!

I love speaking in front of large groups because there are always a handful of people in the audience who legitimately don't think they do this. Not only can you see it on their faces, but you can see the internal dialogue happening inside their head at that exact moment.

"Talk to myself? Are you kidding me, dude? Only crazy people talk to themselves. I'm not crazy. You're crazy, asshole! Talk to myself? Give me a break! This is ridiculous! I wonder what I should eat for dinner?"

Whether you want to admit it or not, you talk to yourself. Hell, you may be just like me and have conversations out loud with yourself.

Here is another spoiler alert. This is a bold assumption, but I feel comfortable saying this because you're a human being, There are times, maybe even a lot of times, when that internal conversation — that voice inside your head — is negative, defeating, and simply not nice. Even the most positive person in the world has destructive thoughts creep in from time to time. They show up in different ways, but a lot of times, it's in the form of an excuse.

"I can't do that ... I'm too out of shape." Or *worse ... "I'm too fat."*

"I can't do that ... I'm not smart enough." *Or worse ... "I'm stupid."*

"I can't do that ... I'm not talented enough." *Or worse ... "I suck."*

It happens. For some people, it happens a lot.

We have to stop that death spiral because if we hear those negative words enough, we will start believing the lies. We have to talk to ourselves positively. In an empowering way. In a nice way.

I'm not asking you to summon your inner Stuart Smalley, the loveable character played by comedian Al Franken on *Saturday Night Live*. Do you remember this guy? He would stare into a mirror, wearing a knitted cardigan and pastel shirt, and say *(with a lisp)*, "I'm going to have a great show today because I'm good enough … I'm smart enough … and doggone it, people like me."

It's funny.

I laugh every time I watch it on YouTube.

But he was onto something. His fictitious TV show, *Daily Affirmations with Stuart Smalley*, was all about talking positively to yourself and giving yourself little reminders that you are special.

Because here is one more spoiler alert: you *are* special. We're all special. We're all masterpieces — one-of-a-kind and rare. There has never been — and there never will be — another person exactly like us. Have you heard this before? *(If your answer is no, please re-read Chapter 1.)*

We have to be intentional about reminding ourselves of that truth. *(And it is the truth.)*

Affirmations were a game-changer in my turnaround.

Stuart Smalley on *Saturday Night Live* was funny and silly. When I started intentionally talking to myself in an empowering way, I didn't feel silly. I felt like a badass.

It took some practice to become efficient in my daily affirmations. I wasn't good at it. Okay, maybe I did feel a little silly. I mentioned earlier in the book that I never embraced this practice when I was doing Hal Elrod's *Miracle Morning*. I think that all stemmed from the fact I didn't know what the hell I was doing.

In Chapter 6, I discussed Napoleon Hill's road map for autosuggestion. Hal models the idea of affirmations after that. It revolves around saying out loud what you want, why you want it, and what you will do to obtain it.

I'm not saying his approach is wrong, but it wasn't impactful for me.

I needed to remind myself I was a one-of-a-kind masterpiece. I needed to write down powerful reminders I was different, and I was special.

I took out my journal and wrote "Truths and Affirmations" in the middle of a blank page. I made a mind-mapping cloud around those three words. Then, I drew arrows from that cloud with a bold statement at the end of each one.

Here are a few of my affirmations:

- I AM a warrior
- I DO live on purpose
- I AM worthy
- I AM extra, and that is not a bad thing
- I deserve all of God's blessings
- Be kind today
- I AM fearless

I made a list of reminders of who I truly am: "I DO love hard," "I get shit done," "I DO leave the moment/situation better than I found it."

I listed visions of where I wanted to go and who I wanted to become: "I WILL succeed," "I WILL break through," "Fear will NOT cripple me."

I included a handful of things I strive to accomplish every day, using the powerful concept of being (instead of just seeming): "Be bold," "Be weird," "Be kind."

Then, I focused on the truths we all tend to forget from time to time: "I deserve all of God's blessings," "I decide my vibe," "I AM enough."

After making my list of affirmations, I read them every day in a very intentional way. I would start somewhere on "my cloud" and read every affirmation/truth in clockwise order. I would find a deliberate rhythm as I read each one. When I got back to the start, I would jump around on the list, reading each affirmation faster and faster. When I got to one that spoke to my soul that day (e.g., "*I DO make the important things important*"), I would slam my journal closed. It was like I was telling myself: "Hell, yeah! Let's ride!"

I would do this every day. Along with intentional prayer, these truths and affirmations became the cornerstone of #myonething. I started to believe in myself again. It was like jet fuel on my campfire.

I also realized this practice kept me from telling myself destructive lies. I didn't have time for that counterproductive nonsense anymore. Any time that head trash would present itself, I would lean on my truths and affirmations. If something didn't go my way, I reminded myself that "I am NOT perfect," and "Failure is a good thing." When I got knocked down, I reminded myself that "quitting is not an option." When the darkness crept in, I would remind myself that "Love wins."

Eventually, there was an equal and opposite reaction to those negative thoughts because if we hear our truths and affirmations enough, we're going to start believing them with all of our heart and soul.

# 24

## Lesson 8: Pray like Mr. Rogers.

I f you don't have a relationship with God, this might not be your favorite chapter in the book. Here is my promise, though, I will not
shove religion down your throat, and I won't start banging on my
Bible, condemning you to eternal damnation. I'm sure there is a Bible
verse that cautions against judging others. I live by that. You'll get zero
judgment from me regarding faith, or anything else, for that matter.
What's that old saying? Throwing stones? Glass house? Don't do it?

Speaking of Bible verses, I only have one memorized. It's Matthew
7:7: *Ask, and it shall be given to you; seek, and you shall find; knock, and it
shall be opened unto you. (There is still an outside chance that I screwed it up.)*

My point: I have zero credibility to lecture you about God or faith or
spirituality. I simply want to share the huge role that intentional prayer
played in my journey.

Let me frame this. When I was in college, I opened my heart to
Jesus. A girlfriend of mine *(shout out to Heather Dunavin)* shared with
me her spiritual beliefs, which slightly cracked the door to my faith.
I remember getting very angry and defensive. To keep the "door"
metaphor going — it was at church a few weeks later when God completely kicked that door open.

It was during a baptism ceremony, and the pastor reminded the con-
gregation, "You don't have to be baptized to accept Jesus Christ as your
Lord and Savior. You don't have to sign a piece of paper or stand up

and announce it at the top of the lungs. You're more than welcome to do that," he said, "but all it takes is for you to open up your heart — you can do it sitting right where you are today – and acknowledge and give thanks that God sent his only Son to die on the cross for our sins."

At that moment, my spiritual relationship with Christ was born. Based on what I've been taught and what I believe, that bond can never be severed. Once He's in your heart, the relationship is eternal — no matter what kind of stupid shit you do or say.

But one thing I have learned since turning my life over to Christ is that we can fall out of fellowship with Him. Sin can't destroy the relationship, but it can compromise that fellowship.

That's where I was when Mr. Rogers came into my life. It was actually Tom Hanks, portraying the incredible Fred Rogers in the movie *A Beautiful Day in the Neighborhood,* who rocked my spiritual world.

When I saw the film, I was completely out of fellowship with God. I couldn't even pray because I felt so unworthy. Every time I tried to have a conversation with God, I was overcome with guilt. I would whisper things to myself, like:

"Why would God listen to *me?*"

"Why would He love *me?*"

"I'm not worthy of His kindness and grace!"

*A Beautiful Day in the Neighborhood* opened my eyes and revealed I was praying wrong.

Now, it's important to know there is not a right or wrong way to pray. It's a personal thing. That movie made me realize I was praying wrong ... for me, and I was selfish when I prayed. I made it all about myself.

"God ... I need this. Lord ... help me with that. Bless me. Forgive me."

Mr. Rogers prayed differently.

In the movie, Tom Hanks ... er ... Mr. Rogers kneels next to his bed with his prayer list, and he begins praying for people by their first and last names. He doesn't say why he's praying for Sam Smith or Debbie

Jackson. He just says their full names — in an almost-mantra. There is a cadence to the way he says the names.

I was immediately intrigued.

So, I started writing down my prayer list. My family was at the top — Crash, Ily, my wife, my parents. Then I listed close friends who were struggling. I remembered seeing posts on social media asking for prayers. I added those, too. I had a solid list.

Then, I prayed like Mr. Rogers. I took the emphasis off me and focused on these twenty-five to thirty people on my prayer list. Again, I said their first and last names out loud. If I knew they needed a few extra prayers that day due to travel or a follow-up at the doctor, I made it a point to recognize that need. Then I got right back into my cadence.

It's kind of hard to explain until you do it yourself, but I found this powerful rhythm that calmed me. It was almost like having a conversation with God while in the middle of a meditation studio.

I instantly loved it, and I became intentional about doing it every day. It was #myonething for several months. I went from struggling to pray to loving it and craving it. All it took was stepping out of the spotlight and putting the emphasis on others.

But that's not the end of the story. Prayer started to be a lot more impactful for me, especially when I began praying for strangers.

Here's an example:

An acquaintance of mine, who I'm now friends with on Facebook, posts about her sick dad. "Please pray for my dad. He was recently diagnosed with Stage 4 colon cancer."

A little less extreme example, "Prayers for my husband … he's quitting his job and finally chasing his dream."

When I would see these posts — and once I started paying attention, I was seeing them *all the time* — I'd ask for the first and last names of the person needing the prayers. I'd ask in the comments of the post. I'd also explain why I wanted to know, citing Mr. Rogers and my new way of praying. They responded with the name and genuine appreciation.

Real quick … I have some head trash about the phrase, "I'm praying for you."

I hate to be cynical about prayer, but I think much of it is just lip service. People say it, but are they doing it? I know these people mean well, but I question if they're saying a specific prayer for their friend's third cousin who just broke up with her boyfriend.

Here is some heavy, behind-the-curtain radical honesty.

When people would tell me they were praying for me, I'd think one of these three self-defeating phrases:

- "Yeah, right" *(with a quick roll of the eyes)*
- "Sure, you are" *(with a hint of sarcasm)*
- "Why?"

Now, I know this comes from a place of self-deprecation, but it was genuine. I didn't feel worthy of anyone else's prayer, so why would they waste time praying for me?

I didn't want anyone feeling that way when I told them I was praying for *them*. I didn't just want to say it like that. To check that box. I didn't want to bring attention to myself by leaving a "praying for you" comment on their social media post.

I wanted them to know I was adding their name — or their loved one's name – to my prayer list. I tried to leave zero doubt.

When I started praying like this … my life completely changed. I was back in fellowship with God.

# 25

## Lesson 9: Make one person's day.

I have four constants on my To-Do List.

Every day, I write three things on the right-hand side of the page, and one thing across the top.

On the side, I write:

- Make one person's day
- Do one thing that scares me
- Don't give an eff *(I actually write out the word, but I promised my mom I wouldn't include the F-word in this book)*

Then, across the top of the page, I put my intention for the day. That is usually a call to action *("Focus")*, a challenge *("Put others first")*, or a powerful reminder to myself *("I'm a badass")*.

After that, I write what I want to accomplish the rest of the day, like a typical To-Do List.

Here is my thought process on writing those four things daily. If I can accomplish those things — and nothing else — it's still a successful day.

In his legendary speech on the ESPY stage, Coach Jim Valvano — dying from cancer that had infiltrated his body — shared a similar recipe for success.

He said:

*To me, there are three things we all should do every day. We should do this every day of our lives. No. 1 is laugh. You should laugh every day. No. 2 is think. You should spend some time in thought. No. 3 is you should have your emotions moved to tears, could be happiness or joy. But think about it. If you laugh, you think and you cry, that's a full day. That's a heckuva day. You do that seven days a week, you're going to have something special.*

If I can make one person's day ... success. If I can do one thing that scares me ... success.

The powerful part about being intentional and doing these two things daily, I never mark them off my list. If I finish editing a podcast or schedule next week's guests for my radio show, I'm quick to take a pen and mark through those action items.

I never mark through "Make someone's day" or "Do one thing that scares me."

Why?

Because that's the beauty of those two charges.

Let's focus on making someone's day.

How would I ever know if I made someone's day? How would I know if I accomplished that goal? Sure, I've had people say those words to me — "you made my day" — but I can't confirm or deny if that's true. I usually get that response after a small act of kindness. For some reason, I quickly downplay it. I think, *How in the world could that have made their day?*

Putting that on my To-Do List reminds me to put others before myself and be kind. It forces me to stay aware of those kinds of opportunities. I don't necessarily buy a stranger's groceries every day or even kick-start the popular "Pay It Forward" initiative at a drive-thru.

I can't believe I'm about to admit this. Did you know there was a time in my life where I struggled with the concept of kindness? Before you think I'm a horrible person, let me explain.

It was after I was introduced to a wonderfully great initiative called "Random Act of Kindness Week." The name speaks for itself — it's a call to action to show kindness, in some capacity, for seven consecutive days. There is a foundation in Denver that spearheads this directive. Its charge: *Take this week to step out of your normal routine or comfort zone and attempt a new random act of kindness each day of the celebratory week.*

I thought it was profound, so I wrote a general blog post about it in 2012. I wanted to inspire others to embrace this endeavor.

I encouraged people to:

- Do something nice for someone you don't know,
- Make a new friend, and
- Give sincere compliments to everyone you meet.

The only problem was, at that point in my life, I didn't walk the walk. I may have thrown around an extra compliment or two, smiled a little more, or told a buddy how much I valued his friendship, but I can honestly say I was sitting firmly on the kindness sidelines.

Though I wrote about it in 2012, I didn't bother to jump in with both feet until 2014.

That's why when I added "Actively Participate in Random Act of Kindness Week" to my life list. I looked up the dates for the next calendar year, marked it on my calendar, and then completely forgot about it.

On Feb. 10 of 2014, I received a reminder notification on my phone: *Happy RAK Week!*

It was here, and I was unprepared.

That sounds kind of strange, huh? Unprepared to show kindness? Yep! Guilty!

I was at a complete loss about what to do. At one point, I even asked myself, "What *is* kindness?" You would have thought that someone told me C-A-T now spelled dog. I sat at my desk, stared at the floor, and hoped for all the answers to magically appear.

I sat there for a long time. No magic.

I re-read my 2012 blog post, but the calls to action were vague (e.g. *"Give generously," "Make a new friend," "Say something nice."*)

Confession: It confused me even more.

Then, I prayed: "Heavenly Father, hi, I don't mean to be an idiot, but I need you to open my heart and educate me about kindness. Show me how you want to use me this week."

I looked up from the floor, and I heard a profound whisper, "How do you experience kindness? What has to happen in your life to feel kindness from another person?"

Then the whisper turned into a loud, stern command, "Start. There. Idiot."

So, I did.

I put together a seven-day plan of attack and executed it:

## *MONDAY*

Reach out to someone who positively impacted my professional career; express my appreciation for how they influenced my life.

*My RAK:* I sent e-mails to two men who gave me the chance to live out my dream of coaching college football. Everett Todd hired me as a volunteer coach at Blinn College in 2001. Mike Sinquefield hired me as recruiting coordinator at TCU three years later.

I told both, "I know it might sound a little weird, but I wouldn't be where I am today without YOU! Thank you!"

## *TUESDAY*

Let someone know they're in my prayers.

*My RAK:* I reached out to a high school buddy and his wife. Their four-year-old son, Jackson, was in a backyard brawl with leukemia. I'd been receiving his updates on Facebook, and his strength and courage inspired me. I wanted his parents to know that prayers were coming their way.

I also shared a wonderfully great story of another family friend whose granddaughter stood toe-to-toe with cancer and whipped its butt. I told them I thought it was important for them to hear stories like that.

## WEDNESDAY

Do something for a complete stranger.

*My RAK:* I bought groceries for a random person.

Confession: I strategically picked this person because her basket was pretty light. I wanted to do something nice and unexpected for someone without taking out a loan. So I purchased some milk, creamer, bananas, a Valentine's card, and some other things.

"I'd like to buy your groceries today," I said.

"I've heard of this. Pay it forward, right?" the lady asked.

I handed her one of my business cards. On the back, I had written "Pay. It. Forward." I also wished her a happy Random Act of Kindness Week. She was very appreciative, and she promised she would bless someone else.

## THURSDAY

Let my family know how much I care.

*My RAK:* I sent flowers to my sisters with a simple note expressing how much I loved them. They are such amazing sisters. I told them I don't tell them that enough.

## FRIDAY (Valentine's Day)

Do something nice for my spouse.

*My RAK:* I played hooky from work and gave my wife an entire day to herself. She could do anything she wanted to do while I held down the fort with the kiddos. I try to give her a couple of hours during the week for "Mommy Day Out," but life sometimes throws a wrench into our plan.

She wrote a Facebook message, "There were no roses delivered to me today, no sparkling jewelry, and no crazy stuffed animals, but I got the best Valentine's day gift I could ever receive. My honey took off work today, and took the kids and gave me a full day to myself!! Can I say I have the most AMAZING hubby ever? So I grabbed my yoga mat, a good read and my breast pump! Ha! Sorry if that's TMI (shrug) but a baby's got to eat! ... And headed out! Feeling refreshed!"

## SATURDAY

Embrace the power of presence.

*My RAK:* My mom has a ninety-year-old cousin who lives in Glen Rose. I spent a little over an hour with her on Saturday morning discussing local politics and family history. She is sharp, funny, and opinionated — all the things that I miss in my two grandmothers.

As I was leaving, we decided it would be nice to do it again soon. She promised to remember to offer me coffee next time.

## SUNDAY

Express gratefulness to my parents.

*My RAK:* I simply wrote my parents a thank you note — expressing my appreciation for them being the greatest parents (and grandparents) in the world. I closed my note by writing, "I love you guys so much. I never want you to question my gratefulness."

- - -

I realized throughout this particular week of kindness that I didn't do this enough. For some tragic reason, it is out of my normal routine and outside my comfort zone. For me, to show kindness *was* random.

That endeavor made me realize it's not that difficult to step out of the spotlight and put emphasis on others. That's all kindness is — putting others before yourself.

After those seven days of executing my plan of attack, I made a vow to myself to remove the "randomness" from my acts of kindness. I promised myself to be more intentional about it. I started writing "Make one person's day on my To-Do List."

It could be a note, e-mail, or letter.

It could be a kind word or a smile.

It could be a helping hand for someone who needs it.

It could be five minutes of my undivided attention.

How do you accomplish this? Just start! Do something kind for another person *right now!* I promise it will completely change your mindset and positively impact your day.

Then what? Do it again tomorrow.

If you're feeling extra, follow my lead and write "make someone's day" on your To-Do List. Make kindness a priority. See if you start looking for opportunities to accomplish that goal throughout your day.

That's exactly why I write those three words on the right side of my To-Do List. Every day, I want to stay keenly aware of making that happen. I'm not paying off someone's mortgage or looking for the chance to save a toddler from a burning building. I'm simply pulling my head out of the sand and taking off the blinders. A non-cliche example: I'm turning off my albatross of a cell phone and paying attention to the world around me. If I see an opportunity to be kind — I pull the trigger.

Theodore Roosevelt said it best, "Do what you can, with what you have, where you are."

# 26

*Lesson 10: Do one thing that scares you.*

*D*amn it!
I haven't introduced the villain for this book yet. I've never written a book, but I know there is supposed to be a bad guy. I recently read Donald Miller's book *Building a StoryBrand,* and he drives this point home. He reminds his readers that every story needs a villain. That is the source of the conflict. That is one of the most important characters in any story.

He wrote:

> *The villain is the No. 1 device storytellers use to give conflict a clear point of focus. Screenwriters and novelists know the stronger, the more evil, the dastardly the villain, the more sympathy we'll have for the hero and the more the audience will want them to win in the end.*

The example he shared in his book: *How sympathetic would Batman be without the Joker? Luke Skywalker without Darth Vadar? Harry Potter without Voldemort? Superman without kryptonite?*

When I read this, I knew who my bad guy was in *Tacos and Chocolate.* Spoiler alert: He's your villain, too.

Cue the sinister music and the dramatic lighting. Almost every day, they enter from stage left in all their glory, walking directly to the center of the stage and giving us the middle finger.

"Ladies and gentlemen, put your hands together for our comfort zone!"

He flashes that smile. You know the one. The smile that says, "I own your ass. You. Are. Mine."

I hate that smile.

I hate my comfort zone.

He's an asshole. *(For the ladies reading this book, she's a heartless bitch.)*

Why? Because our comfort zone is the demon that paralyzes us. He keeps us from making changes in our lives — big or small. He's a dream killer. He coined the phrase, "I'll just do it tomorrow," and encourages us to use it every day.

Let's remove the persona and break down our comfort zone for what it represents.

Our comfort zone is safe and familiar. There are no surprises when we're in our comfort zone — no unexpected missteps or setbacks. Failure is infrequent when we're operating in our comfort zone.

Sounds magical, right?

It sounds tragic. That is why I write "do one thing that scares me" on my To-Do List every day. Eleanor Roosevelt inspired me to do that. She said, "Do one thing every day that scares you."

There is zero ambiguity there.

She has another great quote about fear that complements her iconic challenge. She said, "You gain strength, courage, and confidence from every experience in which you really stop to look fear in the face. You are able to say to yourself, 'I lived through this horror. I can take the next thing that comes along.' You must do the thing you think you cannot do."

Speak it, Eleanor!

I firmly believe that our comfort zone is a dangerous place to be. It will eventually rob us of our joy, crush our souls, and destroy our sense of adventure.

Real estate icon and motivational speaker, Brian Buffini did a wonderfully great podcast about living a life of freedom. He emphasized being flexible to reach that summit. He discussed why we're so rigid and why we get so stuck to lay the foundation for his philosophy.

Buffini got scientific early in this podcast. He dropped the term "homeostasis" on me, which was way over my head. After he shared the definition, I was even more confused.

Homeostasis is the tendency toward a relatively stable equilibrium between interdependent elements, especially as maintained by physiological processes. (*Cue my eyes glazing over, just like they did in 9th-grade science class.*)

Thank goodness he dumbed it down. He used the example of a homing pigeon to illustrate how homeostasis drives our behavior. He said, "Homing pigeons are trained — no matter what they do or where they are or where they're released from, they're trained to go back from where they came from. Human beings have this in spades. We desire to go back to what we know — to what is familiar — to where we feel safe."

He was quick to point out that safe does not mean safety. It means what we know. Even if it's a bad situation — it's what we know.

Buffini said, "We go to what we know because it gives us safety … it gives us confidence … it gives us security. Even if it's bad."

He gave examples of abusive relationships, where the person being abused returns to the destructive relationship — because that's what they know.

"We have to understand that no matter what it is, we have a built-in, anti-growth, anti-development gene inside us," Buffini explained during the podcast. "That's when you try something new, when you develop a new habit, there is an old habit screaming louder to come back. Homeostasis is the single biggest enemy to personal growth and development."

Science wants us to stay in our comfort zone. It doesn't want us to climb out on that limb. We're comfortable with our arms wrapped around the trunk of that metaphorical tree. That's what we know.

That's why we have to be intentional about stretching ourselves and getting comfortable being uncomfortable. That is why I write "do one thing that scares me" on my To-Do List every day. By nature, I'm not a scared person, but I want to stay intentional about facing my fears. I never want my comfort zone — the villain in most people's stories — to win the battle. I don't want him to win the war.

This is an incredible reminder from Max Lucado in his book, *Fearless*:

> *Fear never wrote a symphony or poem, negotiated a peace treaty or cured a disease. Fear never pulled a family out of poverty or a country out of bigotry. Fear never saved a marriage or a business. Courage did that. Faith did that. People who refused to consult or cower to their timidities did that. But fear itself? Fear herds us into a prison and slams the doors.*

Later in the book, Lucado quotes Jesus from Matthew 8:26: "Why are you afraid?"

That's the best question of all.

Are we scared of success? Are we scared that we truly are a one-of-a-kind masterpiece? I think a lot of people are.

Author and activist Marianne Williamson said, "Our deepest fear is not that we are inadequate. Our deepest fear is that we are powerful beyond measure. It is our Light, not our Darkness, that most frightens us."

When I was coaching football at Blinn College, I saw this first-hand.

We recruited players who could have played football at big-time college programs. It was primarily their grades and sometimes their off-the-field antics that forced them to go the junior college route after high school.

As I mentioned earlier in the book, all of them dreamed of playing football at a school like the University of Texas, Auburn, or Michigan. They wanted to play on Saturday afternoon with thousands and thousands of screaming fans in the stands and thousands more watching on TV from the comfort of their homes.

Our goal was to help those boys accomplish that goal. We invested in them, especially academically. We pushed them. We held them accountable. But we could only take them so far, and any kind of success off the football field was utterly foreign to many of them.

Some of our players were terrified of success. Like Marianne Williamson said, their deepest fear was that they were powerful beyond measure.

This was never more evident than when we got a call from campus police in the middle of the night. A handful of our guys had broken into the bookstore. I can't remember what they had stolen, probably something silly like candy or Blinn Buccaneer merchandise. Regardless, they were suspended from the football team, kicked out of school, and sent home.

Those boys had their entire future in front of them. The sky was the limit. But as soon as they started to experience the tiniest bit of success, they got scared and did something stupid.

They went back to a place they were highly familiar with — directly behind the eight ball with their back against the wall.

We all do this! We don't necessarily rob a campus bookstore, but we stop as soon as things start going our way. As soon as we begin to experience success, we take our foot off the pedal and slow down.

I've done it. I started writing this book almost eight years ago but stopped (*several times*).

What are we scared of? I think we're afraid to fall off the pedestal. We're terrified that we're going to get to the top, and a strong wind will blow us off, sending us crashing back to reality.

We're scared of looking stupid or silly.

We're scared of being judged.

How do we lean into that fear? How do we push through? Again, we have to get comfortable with being uncomfortable. For me, that's doing something small every day that scares me just a little.

I thought of a handful of appropriate quotes I could share to close this chapter, but I chose this verse from the Erin Hanson poem, *Reverie*. This powerful reminder is just as much for me as it is for you.

*There is freedom waiting for you,*
*On the breezes of the sky,*
*And you ask "What if I fall?"*
*Oh, but my darling,*
*What if you fly?*

# 27

*The moment you accept total responsibility for everything in your life is the moment you claim the power to anything in your life.*
*— Hal Elrod*

This is it. The beautiful red ribbon that I want to tie around *The Tacos and Chocolate Diet.*

My head trash is in overdrive. I'm scared to death to screw this up. I'm worried I'm writing just to fill space. I don't feel like I'm adding any value to this book.

That is me being real.

"Does this really even need a red ribbon?" the demon asks.

"Shut the hell up! Let's ride!" I command.

As I bring this book to a close, I want to share an inspiring perspective and remind you why I wrote this book.

I'll start with the latter.

I wrote this book because we live in a world full of people who use words like "stuck," "stale," "joyless," and "bored" to describe their lives. These people are running on the hamster wheel of life and not going anywhere. They are addicted to social media, and their favorite phrases are, "I'll just do it tomorrow" and "I'm just so busy."

If this sounds like you and you even have the slightest inclination or desire to make a change, I wrote this book to give you hope. I want to inspire you to take action and start living boldly and adventurously. I want to remind you to make the important things important, starting with you.

I shared my story to show you that anyone can take control of their life; you don't have to do anything over-the-top special to make that change. It's not magic or luck. It's simply about being intentional.

I shared ten lessons that worked for me and helped get me to put an emphasis on my emotional, physical, spiritual, and mental well-being.

- Get to the point of enough
- Be able to sleep in a storm
- Make the important things important
- Ask yourself, "What's next?"
- Focus on #myonething
- Count your wins
- Watch how you talk to yourself
- Pray like Mr. Rogers
- Make one person's day
- Do one thing that scares you

– – –

The nice red ribbon wrapped ceremoniously around this package of inspiration is perspective.

In a spiritual sense, it means seeing life from God's point of view. In the Bible, the words "understanding," "wisdom," and "discernment" all have to do with perspective. It also examines the opposite of perspective:

"Hardness of heart"

"Blinded"

"Dullness"

It's the difference between living in the light or walking aimlessly in the dark.

To quote author Andy Andrews again, "Proper perspective about every facet of your existence is only everything."

When my son was three years old, he fell in love with puzzles. Until I bought him a "big-boy" puzzle, I thought he was pretty good at putting them together. (*Confession: I thoroughly enjoyed finishing some of those 300-piece projects all by myself.*)

Once, I worked on a Peanuts puzzle — specifically Charlie Brown's iconic yellow shirt — and I kept thinking about perspective. I guess a puzzle has a way of emphasizing that. Every time I got stuck with a certain puzzle piece, I'd flip it and rotate it — looking at it a completely different way.

I remember sitting alone at the dining room table — working on Snoopy's doghouse — and starting to recognize the importance of perspective in our lives.

I began analyzing general examples regarding perspective.

Do you think you're stressed? Talk to the single mom of three, holding down two jobs so she can put food on the table.

Does your life feel hopeless? Talk to the addict who has relapsed and their family abandoned them.

Do you hate going to work every morning? Talk to the person who can't find a job.

When I'm talking to a business or organization, the audience usually gets it — the glass can be half full *or* half empty. It's their choice.

Then I share personal examples, specifically about having eleven jobs in the eleven years after graduating from college. While most people might look at this as a monumental failure or consider me a loser, I look at my professional run as a victory.

"I wouldn't be where I am today — doing what I love to do — without going on that crazy eleven-year ride," I said to one church group. "I wouldn't have finally embraced my God-given ability to write and inspire others if I would have stayed in one of those unhappy situations."

I explained that without those jobs, I wouldn't be living a bold and adventurous life right now. Without that perspective, I couldn't be comfortable in my own skin and grateful for where I was in life.

— — —

Here is that final story to drive home the power of perspective.

This amazing story involves one of the world's greatest musicians.

The "stunt" was simple but brilliant: Arrange for this world-renowned musician to play in a public place during an inconvenient time and see what happens. The results of this social experiment were profound *and* eye-opening for me.

I'm not exactly sure how or why this 2007 *Washington Post* article presented itself several years after it happened, and I'm not sure how or why it grabbed my attention. I recently stumbled upon it on my Facebook News Feed. The post teetered on the edge of uninteresting and pointless. It was a grainy surveillance camera photo, and the accompanying text read: "A man sat at a metro station..."

I wish I could say my friend sold it with his supplemental comment, but all he wrote was, "This is so awesome. Please take a moment to read."

For some baffling reason, I followed my friend's passive call to action. And I'm glad I did. It *was* awesome!

There was one poignant question — buried right in the middle of the 7,353-word article — that summed up the greatness of this experiment and the powerfulness of the editorial:

> *If we can't take the time out of our lives to stay a moment and listen to one of the best musicians on Earth play some of the best music ever written; if the surge of modern life so overpowers us that we are deaf and blind to something like that — then what else are we missing?*

The musician was Joshua Bell, and he played for forty-three minutes in the lobby of the Metro station in Washington, D.C. Three days before the stunt, Bell — considered "one of the finest classical musicians in the world" — sold out Symphony Hall in Boston. According to the article, decent seats for that performance cost $100.

During morning rush hour in our nation's capital, 1,097 people passed by Bell.

The article explains:

> *Each passerby had a quick choice to make, one familiar to commuters in any urban area where the occasional street performer is part of the cityscape: Do you stop and listen? Do you hurry past with a blend of guilt and irritation, aware of your cupidity but annoyed by the unbidden demand on your time and your wallet? Do you throw in a buck, just to be polite? Does your decision change if he's really bad? What if he's really good? Do you have time for beauty? Shouldn't you? What's the moral mathematics of the moment?*

*The Washington Post* wanted to see if beauty would transcend in an ordinary setting at an inconvenient time.

The results:

- ○ Seven people stopped what they were doing and listened to the performance for at least a minute;
- ○ Twenty-seven people gave money,
- ○ And Bell collected $32.17 The article says, "Yes, some people gave pennies."

That's the humorous part of the story. *(Humorous, like if LeBron James got selected last in a neighborhood pick-up game.)*

Unfortunately, I found some tragic parts that don't go anywhere near funny or ironic. I lean toward profound and eye-opening. I had to share these:

THE TACOS AND CHOCOLATE DIET | 187

## A Ghost Story

Since the experiment was videotaped, you're able to watch Bell's forty-three-minute performance. *The Post* issues a warning, though: It is extremely sad. Even sped up and bundled in a three-minute montage, it's distressing.

The author writes:

> *Even at this accelerated pace, though, the fiddler's movements remain fluid and graceful; he seems so apart from his audience — unseen, unheard, otherworldly — that you find yourself thinking that he's not really there. A ghost.*

Then the most profound phrase of the article is written: "Only then do you see it, Bell is the one who is real. They are the ghosts."

WOW!

Bell expanded on this after watching the video. "I'm surprised at the number of people who don't pay attention at all," Bell said, puzzled. "As if I'm invisible."

It baffled him because: "I was makin' A LOT of noise."

## What We Really Want

The second part of the story I want to share wasn't necessarily tragic, but it slapped me across the face. It piggybacks on Bell's comments above about being invisible.

In another part of the article, Bell explains he had butterflies during the stunt. He said he was a little stressed. This was coming from a world-class musician who has packed concert halls and played in front of royalty across Europe.

Really?

Really.

"When you play for ticket-holders, you are already validated," Bell explained. "I have no sense that I need to be accepted. I'm already accepted. Here, there was this thought: What if they don't like me? What if they resent my presence ..."

Isn't that what we *all* want? To be recognized? To be validated? To be noticed? To be accepted?

If your answer is "no" — then: You. Are. Lying.

Bell said it was an odd feeling, being completely ignored.

Reminder: That's *my* biggest fear of all-time, and I'm a long way from being world class in anything.

This part of the article was a tremendous reminder that we're all human beings with very similar wants and needs.


## Are You Kidding Me?

This is the part of the story that got me. It made me tuck my lips, shake my head, and whisper, "unbelievable."

Every time a child walked past Bell in the Metro station that morning, they tried to stop and watch. And every time, a parent scooted the kid away.

The article shared a specific moment to drive this disturbing point home. It was about Sheron Parker and her three-year-old son, Evan.

The article says: "You can see Evan clearly on the video. He's the cute black kid in the parka who keeps twisting around to look at Joshua Bell as he is being propelled toward the door."

Evan's mom, who said she was rushed for time, moved between her son and Bell – blocking her toddler's line of sight. As they leave the lobby, Evan can be seen "craning" to get a look at the world-class violinist.

WOW!

The article referenced poet Billy Collins. He once expressed that all babies are born with a knowledge of poetry, because the mother's heartbeat is in iambic meter. "Life slowly starts to choke the poetry out of us," Collins said. The article was implying that it may be true with music, too.

The article ends just like it started, very matter-of-factly. It stirred something inside of me, though. I didn't realize what it was until I skimmed the editorial again to write this last chapter.

It was the question The Post writer asked: "What else are we missing?"

Those five words capture the essence of this stunt. It is what makes it impactful and relevant. It makes me want to start answering that rhetorical question and start doing something about it.

That "something" is simply opening my eyes and ears and paying attention to the little things. It's all about perspective.

Not to completely dumb this down, but the infamous quote from Ferris Bueller has stuck with me since I was introduced to Joshua Bell *(pop culture meets classical music)*: "Life moves pretty fast. If you don't stop and look around once in a while, you could miss it."

# Epilogue

So, I guess I've finally reached the point of the book where I *have to* explain the title, huh?

If you still think *The Tacos and Chocolate Diet* is a fad diet — like Atkins, South Beach, or Paleo — I did a horrible job writing this book *Tacos and Chocolate* is a lifestyle book created around my journey. It's my story, but it is designed to give *you* hope, inspire *you* to live a bold, adventurous, and intentional life, and remind *you* to make the important things important, starting with *you*.

Here is how tacos and chocolate fit into my story.

They accidentally became a staple of my diet in my mid-forties. First, I was introduced to a gluten-conscious diet. There wasn't a sign from God. It was kind of anti-climactic. I had friends who had cut gluten out of their diet, and I liked how they physically looked. So, I decided to try it.

Looking good naked has always been a high priority in my life. If cutting wheat out of my diet would help me accomplish that goal ... let's ride. And yes, I assumed these gluten-free friends of mine looked good without their clothes on.

I didn't know what the hell gluten was.

Here is the formal definition from the Celiac Disease Foundation:

> *Gluten is a general name for the proteins found in wheat (wheatberries, durum, emmer, semolina, spelt, farina, farro, graham, KAMUT® khorasan wheat and einkorn), rye, barley and triticale – a cross between wheat and rye.*

My favorite part of the definition: "Gluten helps foods maintain their shape, acting as a glue that holds food together." Sounds delicious!

Now, at this point of the story, it's important to know I had already stopped drinking alcohol by the time I went gluten-conscious.

I was introduced to many who had stopped drinking or never drank. Most who had stopped drinking were forced to by their demons, but I was drawn to their willpower and ability to be confident and comfortable without a drink in their hand. That planted the seed for me. Then, I had my ah-ha moment. I went to a house concert with my wife. One of my all-time favorite singers and songwriters, Drew Kennedy, was playing in a friend's living room. House concerts are an incredible way to experience music. If you haven't been to one — do it!

I guess I thought it would be a good idea to celebrate the evening by playing "What's at the Bottom of this Bottle of Jameson." I drank half the bottle. I didn't enjoy the show because I was drunk. And the next day, I was a mess.

My wife had to work, and I assumed daddy duty with my two kiddos. I failed miserably that day. I couldn't function. I couldn't engage. I laid on the couch and tried not to throw up. My kids ripped up my Father of the Year application right in front of me. So I decided to stop drinking. And I did — game changer.

From a "try to look good naked" standpoint, I saw immediate results — especially through my mid-section. I still wasn't ready for my Calvin Klein photoshoot, but remember that wasn't my ultimate goal.

I was off the booze when I decided to cut gluten out of my diet. Now, it's important to say this was a choice. I realize there are an estimated 3 million people in this country suffer from celiac and are forced to cut gluten out of their diet. Some of my friends were in this camp. I simply liked how they looked and claimed to feel.

There was a particular time when gluten punched me in the nads.

Crash and I were driving back from a baseball tournament in the Dallas area. We stopped at Buffalo Wild Wings on the way home for a quick dinner and watched the Frogs play football on TV.

We ordered water and a couple of appetizers for our dinner. We opted for one of those giant pretzels and fried pickles. I guess we'd had our fill of protein for the day. I'm disgusted to say I ate 80 percent of that giant pretzel.

I didn't think anything of it as I shoved the warm dough into my mouth, but the following day I felt like I was run over by an Auntie Anne's truck. I woke up feeling sluggish and completely hungover. I felt as if I drank enough booze to kill a small farm animal. I was hurting, and I did not like it.

I immediately accused the pretzel for my faux hangover. I guess it could have been the fried pickles, but I convicted the brown, twisty, lightly salted bread before we could even go to trial.

That's when I drew a hard line in the sand and cut gluten out of my diet. No more. See ya. Bye.

Well, kind of.

I labeled myself "gluten conscious" because I wasn't going to read every label of everything I put in my mouth. Did you know soy sauce has gluten in it? Neither did I, but I wasn't going to go that extreme.

I also wasn't going to interrogate every waiter or waitress about how their gluten-free options were prepared. I know people that blow up like a fart-filled balloon if their food is cooked in the same pan as the gluten-loaded alternative.

If I accidentally got some wheat or rye, it wasn't the end of the world. If I chose to eat one Oreo, which is packed full of gluten, I wasn't going to beat myself up.

I was and am "gluten conscious."

The main things that I cut out of my diet were:

- Bread
- Pasta
- Flour tortillas
- Doughnuts (*I LOVE glazed doughnuts; I could probably eat a dozen by myself if I was left to my own devices*)
- Pizza
- Pastries and baked desserts

That meant no more bun on my hamburgers. No more spaghetti or enchiladas. No more Meat Lovers Pizza. No more cake or pie. No more hot and sugary goodness of glazed doughnuts. I'd already stopped drinking beer, and that's allegedly one of the toughest things for people to give up.

It was still difficult at first, though. Mainly because I was ignorant. I didn't realize the crazy number of gluten-free options and alternatives out there in the world. FYI: I'm not going to swear that these gluten-free items are better than the gluten-packed options, but it's not like eating cardboard. (*A lot of people think that.*)

To help get educated, I leaned on a couple of friends who were forced to go gluten-free because of celiac. These are the before-mentioned fart-filled balloons.

The best tip they gave me: Eat more corn. Because unbeknownst to me at the beginning of this nutrition adventure, there is no gluten in corn.

I was told that corn was my new BFF.

That opened up a whole new world for me, and that is when tacos became a staple of my diet. In hindsight, it was an easy transition. I started eating crunchy tacos or street tacos. No more flour tortillas. No more burritos. When I got fajitas, I chose corn tortillas. I could eat all the beans and rice my heart desired.

Oh … and I could eat the hell out of some chips and salsa. No gluten!

"Would you like some more chips?" the nice waitress asked.

"Since I can't eat seventy percent of the things on your menu, yes, please."

"*¿Como?*" *the waitress asked.*

I'm endorsing Mexican food because I effing love it, and I could eat it every day. Another reason, when I started this diet, I *was* eating it every day. Since most fast-food places — especially hamburger joints and sandwich shops — put an emphasis on the bread, those are tough places to find gluten-free options. I've been known to get a burger without the bun, but that means it *does* come with a fork, which is not conducive to eating on the go.

That is one downside to this gluten-conscious lifestyle.

Quick rabbit hole: I don't like to eat. The only reason I eat is, so I don't die. If I had one superpower, it would be I didn't *have* to eat. It just slows me down. With this awesome, time-saving superpower, I *could* eat if I wanted to have a delicious meal, but I wouldn't need food to survive.

The reason I brought this up now is I'm usually eating while doing six other things, and I'm usually rippin' and runnin' my way to do something else. Being gluten-conscious makes that difficult.

Through all of this, I've realized why two-thirds of adults in the United States are overweight or obese. It comes down to convenience. We love our fast food. We're addicted to the drive-thru.

Trust me; I get it. "Give me my food as fast as possible and make it easy to eat while I'm driving down the road. I have shit to do!"

When you cut gluten out of your diet, you're forced to do things differently. It's not difficult by any stretch of the imagination, but it's not convenient. The crazy part about that statement for a lot of people, removing that convenience immediately makes them think it's hard to do.

It simply means you have to plan, be flexible, and know how to adjust on the move when a menu is packed full of bread options.

So, give me a couple of tacos with a side of taco.

Other things that started to become a staple of my diet were:

- French fries (potatoes do not have gluten)
- Chinese food (rice does not have gluten)
- Fruits and vegetables (no gluten)

The great part about all of this, was seeing positive side effects in my physique. I was losing my newfound baby fat around my midsection.

Now, it's important to know that this diet was getting built on a solid foundation. I didn't go from the shittiest eater in the history of forever to gluten-conscious. Not counting my college diet of Snickers, Big Mac, Coke, and Miller Lite, I watched what I put in my body.

At the time that I cut out gluten, I was doing the following things:

- I only drank black coffee
- I had completely eliminated soda
- I drank a lot of water *(Game-changing decision: I started making sure that I drank a big glass of water before my morning coffee)*

- I limited my fast food (*I love Whataburger*)
- I was intentional about eating breakfast

I wasn't obese or even overweight. I was just soft around the midsection. I didn't love how I looked naked, but nothing was working. That's when I realized I would have to be a little more radical with my nutrition.

Spoiler alert: Father Time is an asshole.

So yes, I started eating a ton of tacos, and my body started to change. It wasn't over-the-top drastic, but I was happy with the results.

"Hey, what about the chocolate? Remember, the name of this book is *Tacos AND Chocolate Diet?*" you ask.

"I remember, impatient reader! I was just waiting for the right moment to drop some science on you."

Here is your science lesson. This is copy and pasted from the American Heart Association website:

> *When you eat carbs, your body breaks them down into simple sugars, which are absorbed into the bloodstream. As the sugar level rises in your body, the pancreas releases a hormone called insulin. Insulin is needed to move sugar from the blood into the cells, where the sugar can be used as a source of energy.*

Long story, short… my body was craving sugar. When I cut out bread, flour tortillas, pizza, doughnuts, and baked desserts, my body didn't have those carbs to break down. I was craving sweets.

So, I turned to my fart-filled balloon friends again. I knew they had the answers. "All I want to do is eat an entire wedding cake! I need something sweet! Help!"

"Calm down. Eat chocolate. Most Chocolate doesn't have gluten," my friends said.

After that very-real conversation, I raced to the closest convenience store. I bought the biggest pack of Peanut M&Ms I could find. I devoured it. Then, I bought another pack and ate it, too.

My world completely changed, and I didn't have an intense desire to murder a stranger after they looked at me funny for shuffling along the sidewalk, mumbling "glazed doughnuts … glazed doughnuts."

So that is how the *Tacos and Chocolate Diet* was born.

Recap: I received advice from some friends who lived a gluten-free lifestyle. I focused on eating tacos on corn tortillas and Peanut M&Ms. I started to look better with my clothes off. I decided to give this inspirational memoir an obscure title.

– – –

Since starting this book, I've made additional adjustments to my nutrition. I mentioned in the introduction I tried a plant-based diet. Many people call it a vegan diet, but I thought that sounded kind of pompous and douchey.

I completely cut meat and dairy out of my diet for four months. That included eggs, milk, and cheese. I ate a ton of avocados and beans and vegetables.

I saw an immediate difference, but it wasn't sustainable. It was difficult obtaining calories. Loss of weight followed, and not in a good way. I looked sick.

So, I punted.

I started to incorporate a limited amount of processed meat into my diet, specifically lunch meat, but I left out cheese and milk.

That's where I'm at as I write this book. At forty-six-years old, it's my sweet spot. I won't bore you with all my numbers from my recent physical — you know … blood pressure, cholesterol, blah, blah, blah — but here is a snapshot of the conversation I had with my doctor after my results came back:

"Perfect? Really?" I asked, astonished.

"Would you be willing to be our poster boy for healthy living?" the doctor responded.

"Only if you promise to never do that thing with your finger again!"

# Who the Hell is Drew Myers?

*posts from Defining Audacity blog*

**Author's Note:** *These blog posts were referenced or mentioned throughout this book. I wanted to include the entire blog post. This will give you a better insight into me and what makes me who I am.*

## DEFINING AN ADVENTURE?
*published May 3, 2008*

It's not easy to define the word "adventure."

As I pedaled my mountain bike up 3,000 feet over twelve miles during my recent trip to Colorado — legs and lungs yearning for a quiet vacation on a tropical beach — I wrestled with my own definition.

When I was screaming down the backside of the mountain — dropping 3,000 feet in five miles — I had a pretty good grasp on what I thought an adventure might be.

When you aren't 100 percent sure what's coming around the next corner, whether that's on the side of a mountain or walking down a strange street, you are in the midst of an adventure.

If you apply that definition to my 100-mile bike ride in Colorado, I experienced the adventure of a lifetime. Here's the breakdown: Along with a good buddy of mine from TCU, I rode approximately 100 miles over four days through the mountains of the Centennial State. *(Once again, that's Colorado for those not familiar with obscure state mottos.)* It was a hut-to-hut ride that was highlighted by single-track excursions, nasty climbs, and "hold-on-to-your-hat" descents.

We topped out at 9,300 feet. We battled sand, wind, and altitude. There was a little blood, a lot of sweat, and maybe one tear when the adventure was finally over.

I kept a crude journal that helped keep the adventure in perspective.

After the first day of riding, I wrote, "Adventure ... challenge ... pushing your own physical limits."

If I only knew what the next three days entailed. *(I should have had an idea — before the adventure started, I had to fill out a search and rescue permit just in case they had to air-lift my mangled body off the mountain.)*

I took a couple of spills my first day on the bike — hence the blood. I was acclimating myself with the climbs and new pair of cleated shoes. For all of my non-bike-riding friends ... imagine having your foot duct taped to the pedal of a bike. Now, when you're in the wrong gear on the side of a mountain — which literally keeps your pedals from moving — you have to separate your taped foot from the pedal in order to catch yourself. If you don't, you bust your tail.

Five miles into the ride, I didn't get my foot separated a couple of times and I honestly thought filling out my search and rescue permit was the smartest thing I had done all morning. *(I wish I could say that these "wipe-outs" were worthy of the highlight reel, but I was just falling over.)*

As the day progressed, I got more comfortable and finished extremely strong — a 1.5-mile climb described in our directions as "nastiness." The altitude tested my intestinal fortitude, but I made it to the first hut in one piece.

All part of the adventure.

I was loving it!

– – –

At the start of Day No. 2, I was extremely confident. At the end of the day, I wrote the following phrase in my journal, "Hell came early!"

I was introduced to "hike-a-bike," which is a stretch of the trail that is un-rideable. You literally have to get off your bike and push it. My first "hike-a-bike" was half a mile, straight up the side of a canyon. (*If I failed to mention the rocky terrain, you would miss some of the color from the experience.*)

Other highlights from Day 2: By our own stupidity, we got a little lost. It wouldn't have been too bad if it weren't for the poison ivy and the fact we generated our own "hike-a-bike." We probably took a 3.5-mile detour, with half of it off of our bikes, through the poison ivy capital of Colorado.

(*Needless to say, I was anticipating a trip to the 24-hour clinic after the ride. At this point of the trip, it would have entailed stitches and a steroid shot to combat the poison ivy.*)

As you read this on your computer — the air conditioning sending cold chills down your spine from time to time — this might not sound like fun.

I was having the time of my life.

I was pushing my body harder and longer than I ever thought possible; I was in the middle of some of the most beautiful back country in the world, and I didn't know what was going to be thrown at me next — a true adventure!

– – –

Day No. 3: Best riding of the trip, by far — that was with a ¾-mile "hike-a-bike." (*Please re-read the previous "hike-a-bike" paragraph and add another quarter mile of hell.*) The third day was mostly single-track and a lot of rolling terrain.

Besides getting a lot more confident and aggressive with my riding, I learned a couple of lessons — trust your instincts and live in the moment. The "trust your instinct" lesson was from another minor detour and the "live in the moment" lesson was generated by the 6-mile descent to the hut. (*I had to do everything in my power to not think about riding the same 6 miles uphill the very next morning.*)

One of the highlights of the day was when I bathed naked in an irrigation stream after the ride. (*It was my first bath/shower in 48 hours. That is the only reason I mention it.*)

That night, my buddy and I sat on the porch of the hut (clothes back on) watching the sun race behind one of the canyon walls. That's when I started to get philosophical. I started thinking about my life — specifically where I'd been, where I am now, and mostly about where I'm going. I think the endorphins from the ride – plus the cold water from the irrigation stream — gave my brain a jump-start.

With my mind going 100 mph, it was hard to fall asleep that night.

– – –

Day No. 4: "I wish I had gotten a better night's sleep!"

This was the 3,000-foot climb in 12 miles. It was a little more extreme than that, because during that 12-mile stretch, we went downhill for the most parts of mile seven, eight, and nine.

Once we started up for good, I referred to it as the "NeverEnding Incline." (*If you sing that with the tune from the movie "The NeverEnding Story," it makes the time go by faster.*)

As mentioned before, it was a grind going up, but we were shot out of a gun on the way down — 3,000 feet in 5 miles. As I raced down into the canyon, my main focus was the extreme drop-off within arm's reach, but I also thought about how to make everyone understand this part of the adventure.

Three thousand feet in 5 miles: Take two Sears Towers and stack them on top of each other, connect approximately 25 of those old-school metal slides together — some long, some short, and some curved. Then pour gravel, sand, and dirt from 500 dump trucks down those slides.

Now, it's time to balance on two wheels and point those handlebars towards the bottom.

The instructions we were given read, "Have fun, be careful, and hang on to your hat."

We finished Day 4 at the Gateway Resort, where a hot shower, a real bed, and a decent dinner was waiting for us. (*The dinner aspect would have been a lot more extreme if we hadn't eaten so well on the trip ... brats the first night, BBQ chicken on Day 2, and cheese burgers in Hut No. 3.*)

Reacquainting ourselves with world news — especially Sportscenter — was huge as well.

---

Day No. 5: We were done. We had the option of a different kind of adventure on the fifth day — kayaking, tubing, white-water rafting — but exhaustion had crept in during the night. The real bed, ESPN, and our looming journey back home kept us close to our bungalow. We had a great breakfast before we were shuttled back to our cars.

As I drove down the highway out of Fruita, the small Colorado town where the adventure started, I could see the mountains and canyons we had just conquered.

A sense of pride and fulfillment overtook me.

Was it the hardest thing I had ever done? No ... the marathon still holds that distinction.

Was it the most exciting thing I had ever accomplished? No ... loading everything up and moving to Oregon for a year packed a lot more excitement.

I wasn't chased by a bear or mountain lion. I didn't swim a raging river that was miraculously infested by piranhas. I wasn't forced to battle a forest fire with nothing more than my water bottles.

It was still an adventure, though. One I will never forget.

I boldly did something I never thought of doing, and I quenched my passion for something new and different.

The only remaining question: What's next?

### 

## DEFINING MOMENT:
## WHAT IS THE REAL MEANING OF 'DNF'?
*published April 27, 2009*

D NF is an acronym for "Did Not Finish."
In regards to running, it's unceremoniously placed next to the names of the people who never crossed the finish line of a particular race.

You can usually find this unflattering distinction on the race website and/or buried in the results of the local newspaper.

There are probably thousands and thousands of people who have unintentionally joined this infamous club.

Well, I am NOT proud to say that I'm now an official card-carrying member.

At Mile 24 of the Country Music Marathon in Nashville, I walked off the course and into the medical tent. I didn't take one more step towards completing my third marathon.

My only glimpse of the finish line was through the ambulance window. I was being transported to a Nashville hospital for dehydration. (*Symptoms: Severe cramps, nausea, light-headedness, wounded pride.*)

No cheering crowds during the last .2 miles.

No sense of accomplishment.

No medal around my neck.

It wasn't until I was discharged from the hospital — three hours and two bags of saline later — when the wave of emotions hit me. (*It was like someone wearing out my soul with a baseball bat.*)

I was calling friends and family to let them know that I was fine. (*Very tired, very sore, extremely hungry — but fine.*)

While I was on the phone with my mom, I just started to cry.

All I could think about was "DNF" — not the actual meaning and/or the fact that it would be next to my name forever in the Archived Results on the Marathon website.

I just couldn't stop thinking about what it represented:

- All my hard work over the last 16 weeks was for nothing.
- I set a goal, and I was unable to reach it. (*Probably the hardest thing to swallow.*)

My emotions generated unnerving questions:

- Could I have kept going? (*It was ONLY two more miles!!!!*)
- Did I quit?

- Did I sell myself short?
- What did I do wrong? *(Training? Diet? The way I approached the race?)*

I played back every mile of the race, which kept the questions flowing:

- Too fast in Mile 7 *(WHY?)*
- Let the long hill at Mile 12 get into my head *(WHY?)*
- Not enough fluids after Mile 13 *(WHY?)*
- Mile 16 ... I actually said to myself, "I'm in trouble." *(WHY?)*
- Mile 17 ... started to cramp *(WHY?)*
- Mile 20 ... started to have doubts *(WHY?)*
- Mile 24 ... "Sir, are you OK?" ... "I don't think so."

## WHY DID I SAY THAT?

This was going to be my last marathon. My plan was to break the 4-hour barrier and switch to half marathons, adventure races, and triathlons. The training had taken its toll, and my love of lacing up my sneakers and hitting the pavement was bruised.

I had decided that Nashville was going to be the last time my legs carried me 26.2 miles.

Not finishing EVER crossed my mind, though.

As the warm tears cut through the salt residue on my cheeks, I realized that I HAD to run one more. I couldn't finish my brief "marathon career" with a DNF.

Since I accidentally left my confidence in the back of that ambulance, my doubt made me cry harder. I kept asking myself, "Can I do it again? Can I do it again?"

Well, it's been thirty-two hours since I uttered those four pride-piercing words — "I don't think so" — to the marathon medical staff.

Believe it or not it, the healing process has already started. *(All the encouraging messages I received AND writing this blog post have helped consider-*

*ably, but the fact that I've stopped feeling sorry for myself and I'm now pissed off has changed my focus.)*

I am more motivated than I have EVER been. I've already decided that I am running the Rock 'n' Roll Marathon in San Antonio on November 15th. *(I start training the second week of August ... IN THE HEAT.)*

I will finish!

I will break four hours!

I will make good on all the financial support that I received for Nashville! *(donations to Back on My Feet)*.

As we were packing up to come home from Nashville, I almost threw away my race number. I didn't want to be reminded about that race in any shape, form, or fashion.

Then I remembered what Duke basketball coach Mike Krzyzewski said after the Blue Devils got rolled in the ACC Tournament one year *(109-66 loss to Virginia)*.

After the embarrassing loss, one of his staff members said with good intentions, "...here's to forgetting tonight ever happened." Coach K quickly interjected, "Here's to never forgetting tonight happened. Not ever."

I must never forget about the 10th Annual Country Music Marathon. In the long run, this actually may be the race that ends up defining me.

I whole-heartedly support an organization *(Back on My Feet)* that helps individuals pick themselves up when they stumble, encourages them to dust themselves off, and most importantly, inspires them to keep fighting. If I felt sorry for myself for one more second *(or remained embarrassed and/ or defeated)*, I would be a hypocrite.

I didn't finish the 2009 Nashville Marathon. I'm not proud of that reality, but I've accepted it.

That DNF next to my name stands for "Do Not Forget."

I won't. It's time to get back on my feet and fight.

###

## A FABULOUS FAREWELL ... TO ME!

*published June 6, 2012*

I've told my wife that I want her to have me stuffed when I die.

Oh, yeah...I'm talking taxidermy. She can prop me up in the corner of the living room and dress me in different outfits, according to the season. *(A tacky Christmas sweater in December, a nice pastel tie at Easter, etc.)*

Whatcha think? Awesome, right?

Yeah ... she's not crazy about the idea either.

Confession: I only tell people this, including my wife, to generate an extreme reaction. Most of the time, that reaction is disgust, with a few awkward giggles sprinkled in. *(I think only one person has ever said, "That's cool!")*

The only reason I bring it up right now, I've been thinking about my funeral a lot lately, and I have some legitimate post-mortem requests that I don't want to fall through the cracks.

I've discussed these details with my wife, but I thought a blog post dedicated to this subject would help hold her accountable.

Editor's Note: I am NOT dying and I don't plan on dying anytime soon. But as you know, there are no guarantees about tomorrow.

– – –

It's important to know and understand the M.O. of my funeral: Get people from sadness, to closure, to the after party as fast as possible. I want a few tears and then give them a firm kick in the pants to start living a bold and adventurous life.

Here are the details and the Run of Show:

### ACT I: THE FUNERAL

- Held in church — no funeral home

- NO flowers; in honor of my failed business venture, e-Partners in Giving, I want donations made to Big Brothers Big Sisters in the name of my son, Crash Greer Myers.

- Open casket is a MUST; this is a tribute to all my loved ones who opened their caskets for me. I've thoroughly hated most of the funerals I've ever attended because of this sadistic ritual. I know seeing the deceased one more time gives some people closure, but it's devastating for me. I get closure in other ways. *(Normally sobbing like an idiot.)* Most funerals I attend, I'm forced to stare at the floor the whole time. *(Again, blubbering uncontrollably.)* You'd think I'd opt for NO open casket because of my overwhelming disdain. NOPE! This is my final chance to inflict revenge – not to mention be completely narcissistic. One. More. Time. I'm even going to take it to another level: Tilted casket AND a forced "walk by."

- The funeral will kick off with an acoustic version of "I Can Only Imagine;" I'm thinking a simple bar stool, a guitar and a famous Texas Country Music artist.

- Two friends — two stories; I want a couple of my best friends – Greg and Nick — to tell one story each. I won't go as far to pick the stories, but they better be funny and poignant.

- Black gospel choir sings *Amazing Grace*; I think the robes and a surprise solo in the midst of the second verse will bring the house down. *(Slide show of random pictures can be shown here OR when the choir sings Van Halen's "Right Now" later in the ceremony.)*

- The "sermon" — from a removed third-party; The third speaker will be someone who is somewhat detached from the situation. I need someone who can hold it together and drive home the fact that I'm in Heaven. I want them to share my faith, and the fact I'd embraced Jesus Christ as my Lord and Savior. Random question: Have you ever been to a funeral and thought: "Are we absolutely sure he's in Heaven?" Not at mine.

○ Gospel choir sings *Right Now* with accompanying piano; Reminder: Slide show optional at this point of the funeral.

○ Short message from me played through the loudspeaker; I'll simply thank everyone for coming.

○

Everyone stands and sings *American Pie* together — led by Greg.

## ACT II: THE GRAVESIDE

○ It MUST be raining *(black umbrellas will be supplied to all guests)*; Even if TK needs to keep my body on ice for a couple of weeks, I want there to be a steady shower when they put me in the ground. It adds to the drama. Some people might worry that family and friends won't show back up for a second round of mourning, but it's my goal to make the funeral such a production. Their curiosity and intrigue won't allow them to miss Act II.

○ Read quote by Victor Hugo *(I carried this in my pocket during my first marathon)*; Excerpt: "The bold ones continue. They are eyed by the eagles; the lightning plays about them: the hurricane is furious ... No matter, they persevere."

○ Bagpipes play *Amazing Grace*;

○ Scripture reading *(Philippians 3: 13-14)* "Brothers, I do not consider myself yet to have taken hold of it. But one thing I do: Forgetting what is behind and straining toward what is ahead, press on toward the goal to win the prize for which God has called me heavenward in Christ Jesus."

○ I'm still trying to figure out how a civilian receives a legitimate 21-gun salute. I'm thinking I might have to switch gears and go with fireworks. NOTE: The guests will be able to keep the black umbrellas.

— — —

## ACT III: THE AFTER PARTY

I'm not that concerned about the details of the party — the when, the where, the type of snacks. There just better be one!

My only request: Shiner Bock in a bottle and an unlimited supply of Jameson.

— — —

When I shared this unusual blog post idea with a friend of mine, she said: "It's going to be really weird if something tragic happens to you after you write that."

My response: "Yeah, but at least my funeral won't be boring."

### 

## MY DIRTY LITTLE SECRET...BLOGGING GREATNESS?
*published June 15, 2012*

I recently read that one of the "rules" of creating a great blog was transparency. I feel like I do a pretty decent job of following that rule, BUT … you can always push yourself just a little further, right?

So here goes nothing! *(My wife and my mother just cringed ... in this instance they may be justified.)*

I wanted to share something I wrote almost ten years ago for *Reader's Digest*. It was never published, but I submitted it on a whim. I saw a submission request in the legendary publication, asking for a 300-word essay on your most embarrassing moment. Authors would receive $500 if their story was selected.

I went for it.

I checked my ego at the door and spilled my guts ... literally.

Here's me being completely transparent and hopefully taking my blog to "greatness."

Oh, crap!

The food in college dining halls has a tendency to leave an impression on the students who consume it. For me, it left more of an impression on my boxer shorts.

It was my sophomore year in college, when I experienced the most heart-stopping, blood-rushing-to-my-head embarrassment of my life.

My roommate and I had just returned to our dorm room after typical all-you-could-eat fare. Like many post-cafeteria visits, I was suffering from a small case of gas and proceeded to nonchalantly release it.

This particular time, though — there really is no easy way to say this — I pooped my pants. I stood there with the dumbest look of shock on my face as my underwear filled up like I was a toddler.

"I think I just shit my pants," I said in the calmest of voices.

By the look on my face, my roommate knew I wasn't kidding.

While I stood motionless, my roommate proceeded to laugh hysterically until he was doubled over on the floor, gasping for air.

When he finally caught his breath, he looked back at me. I was still frozen. He started rolling around on the floor again. The tears started flowing as he crawled into the hallway and watched me waddle to the bathroom. As I stood in the shower fully clothed, I could still hear him laughing.

For the next several years, he loved to act out the events of that night, from the stupid look on my face to my infamous words: "I think I shit my pants."

It wasn't until two years ago — almost six years after the incident — that I decided to come clean. *(No pun intended.)* My roommate held that over my head for years and years, threatening to tell my "dirty secret."

I finally decided it wasn't a big deal for a twenty year old to poop his pants.

– – –

**Author's Note:** I let my wife read this post before I published it. She was NOT impressed. She actually said: "Eh..." Her response surprised me a little, and I actually thought about punting — moving it into a folder on my desktop to be hidden forever.

I couldn't figure out if she didn't like the tone, thought I used too many dangling participles OR was embarrassed that I "sharted" before "shart" was a term.

Then she asked me: "Why are you sharing this? Who are you writing for?"

Valid questions.

I thought it was a great time to remind everyone — including myself — why *Defining Audacity* exists.

When I started this blog, I asked myself two questions:

- Am I qualified to start a blog about living a bold and adventurous life?
- Am I qualified to motivate others to live the same way?

My answer was AND still is: ABSOLUTELY! I feel like I personally live a bold and adventurous life, and I want to lead by example.

I feel like the only way I can do that is for the real me to come across — whether I'm wearing my daddy hat, talking about my Live the List Project or being over-the-top transparent. Since I started writing on a regular basis, I've realized that the ONLY thing that differentiates my blog from the other 100 MILLION blogs on the internet is ... ME!

I wrote this in my inaugural *Defining Audacity* post:

Living a bold and adventurous life doesn't mean that I'm climbing Mount Everest or swimming with sharks on a daily basis. It simply means that I'm living life on my terms. I'm putting my faith and my family above all else, and I'm trying to live everyday full throttle — absent of fear and doubt.

To me, living boldly and adventurously also means:

- Playing a key role in raising my son;
- Finally using the gifts that God has blessed me with – writing and inspiring others;
- Refusing to make excuses;
- Not living scared;
- And constantly trying to throw a wrench in the status quo.

As I started to drag my *Reader's Digest* submission to its eternal grave on my desktop, I asked myself what the status quo would do.

Obviously, I did the opposite. *(Sorry, honey!)*

### 

## GETTING PHYSICAL WITH PERFECTION
*published Oct. 8, 2013*

D isclaimer: I KNOW that I'm not going to live forever. In fact, I to-tally realize that after I hit "publish" on this blog post I could...

...get hit by bus;

...suffer a stroke;

...be attacked by killer hornets, or

...explode in a weird farm accident.

So...please know and understand that I'm not declaring my immortality in this 500-word narrative. I'm simply stating a fact:

My doctor said that I was perfect.

I won't bore you with all "my numbers" from my recent physical — you know ... blood pressure, cholesterol, blah, blah, blah — but here is a snapshot of the conversation that I had with my doctor after my results came back:

Me: "Perfect? Really?"

Doctor: "Would you be willing to be our poster boy for healthy living?"

Me: "ONLY if you promise to never do that thing with your finger again!"

Confession: I was pretty stoked to get the results. I didn't think that I was going to "fail," but you never know what a little probing and blood work will uncover. Especially with my family history of heart disease and high cholesterol, I'm always on edge until I get the thumbs-up.

After this physical, I received two thumbs-up.

Yippie!

OK ... OK ... in order to maintain my integrity ... two thumbs-up is ALL I got. Doctor Jellyfinger didn't actually use the adjective "perfect" when he was giving me my results, BUT he did say "keep doing what you're doing."

Confession: That made me happier than him nominating me for The Healthiest Man in the World.

His directions to "stay the course" thrilled me, BECAUSE that meant I could keep....

- Drinking Shiner Bock *(or any cold beer)*;
- Eating Whataburger;
- Salting my food;
- Smoking the occasional cigar;
- Devouring a couple PB&J sandwiches after 11 p.m.;
- Staying up late;
- Pouring myself a glass of Scotch rocks from time to time;
- Treating myself to Mexican food on a regular basis;
- Enjoying my morning cups of coffee;

○ Munching on popcorn *(with extra butter)* at the movie theatre.

That's the fun part of my "diagnosis," but I also knew I had to keep working so those trips through the Whataburger drive-in didn't take me down.

My doctor's orders to "keep on keeping on" humbled me, BECAUSE that also meant I had to keep...

○ Running every day;
○ Drinking lots of water;
○ Limiting the amount of fast food that I eat *(Whataburger is the only regular villain)*;
○ Monitoring my soda intake (I like to keep it around zero);
○ Taking the stairs, instead of the elevator when I can;
○ Looking for parking spots a little further from the front door, and
○ Playing baseball and football with my son

Again, I'm ecstatic that "my numbers" look good as I stare down the barrel of my 40th birthday, but that's not the driving force behind my "healthy" living. You know what motivates me?

1) Being a good example for my kids, and
2) Trying to look good naked.

Perfect answer? I thought so, too.

###

## FIGHT TO THE FINISH:
## DEMONS CAN'T STOP HISTORIC RUN
*published March 4, 2014*

I recently accomplished one of the greatest personal feats of my life — running a marathon in less than 4 hours — and I'm at a complete loss for words.

Complete. Loss.

I know that I want to write something about the amazing experience, but I have no idea where to start. I think it's because I don't know exactly how I'm feeling right now — just sixty hours after crossing the finish line of the The Army Marathon.

Part of me is still trying to process everything.

Part of me is in shock.

Part of me is just happy it's over.

Someone asked me if I was euphoric. Nope.

Someone else asked me if I was relieved. Not particularly.

I guess I'm proud of myself, because I said that I was going to do something and I worked my tail off to make it happen. But pride is a dangerous emotion.

Yay me?

Blah.

As I reflect on the race – which took place on a bitterly cold and windy morning in Central Texas – all I can think about are the poignant conversations that I had with myself over the last five or six miles.

These conversations were extremely loud and exceptionally clear because I was running completely "unplugged." I grudgingly left my headphones in the car, and my running watch was ceremoniously stolen before the race started.

I hadn't run like this in a long time. I felt naked.

But you know what? It's exactly what I needed.

Instead of looking at my watch every three or four minutes – fretting about my pace – or wondering what the next song would be on my I-Tunes, I stood toe-to-toe with some of my inner demons.

And we talked it out like men.

*"It's so cold..."*

*"Stop feeling sorry for yourself — keep running...keep fighting."*

*"I can't feel my fingers and my feet hurt..."*

*"Failure is not an option — not today."*

*"What's the point ... I'm barely moving because the wind is blowing so strong..."*

*"But you ARE moving. Do. Not. Stop."*

*"Maybe I'm not supposed to run marathons..."*

*"This is NOT Nashville. Stay in the moment...fight!"*

As I approached the 24th mile marker, I thought a lot about Nashville — my last attempt to complete a marathon.

I thought about that question that ended my day — only 2.2 miles from the finish line: "Sir, are you OK?"

I thought about my confidence-shattering response: "I don't think so."

Then there was the ambulance that carried me and my disappointment to the hospital. I thought about that, too.

How could I not think about it? That was the last time I had run that far.

But when I hit mile marker No. 24 in the Army Marathon, I just smiled and winked to the running gods. I was feeling strong, and I was focused. I wasn't sure if the 4-hour mark was still doable, but I knew that I was going to finish this 26.2-mile race.

My inner demons had other intentions, though...

*"It's so cold..."*

*"You said you were going to do it ... Do. It."*

*"It's not the right day to break 4 hours..."*

*"The right day? When will it be the 'right' day? Run!"*

*"What if I fail AGAIN?!?!?"*

*"What if you DON'T? What if you break the 4-hour barrier on this crazy, cold day? How sweet will that be?"*

Right in the middle of this internal dialogue, I started to pray. I can't remember the exact point in the race when this happened, but I'm sure my fingers were numb and the 20-mph wind was blowing directly into my face.

I started to express my gratefulness to God. I thanked Him for all the wonderfully great things in my life.

I thanked Him for the love and support of my family and friends. My kids. My wife. My parents and siblings.

I thanked Him for the men and women who have died for my freedom. There were constant reminders about these sacrifices throughout the race. I ran with a countless number of service men and women and their families. A handful of runners were honoring fallen members of the military on their bibs.

I thanked God for my health and the ability to run. I told Him that I realized there are a lot of people in the world who can't OR won't lace 'em up and pound the pavement.

I thanked Him for the oxygen in my lungs and the muscles in my legs.

I thanked Him for my drive and determination.

When I finally reached a turn in the course, I thanked God for the wind at my back and the sensations returning to my fingers.

My demons weren't impressed, though. They refused to give in...

*"Uh, oh ... a cramp..."*

*"Keep running."*

*"It feels like a hot knife in my calf..."*

*"Keep. Running."*

*"What if they get worse..."*

*"You'll keep running and finish."*

*"What's the point..."*

*"You set a goal. Go and get it."*
*"But I'm hurting..."*
*"Seriously?"*

I asked myself that direct and rhetorical question because I thought back to two remarkable gentlemen that I "got to know" during my training for the Army Marathon.

On several of my long training runs, I "met" Cpl. Pat Tillman when I listened to the audiobook *Where Men Win Glory* by Joh Krakauer.

In the midst of my training, I also read *Lone Survivor* and was introduced to the amazing story of Navy Seal Marcus Luttrell.

These two men laid it all on the line for our country. It cost Tillman, a former NFL standout, his life. It cost Marcus Luttrell three of his brothers from Seal Team 10. They were both pushed to the brink of hell to protect our freedom.

All I had was a cramp.

As I ran with pain in my legs, I thought back to everything those guys went through. They were bloody, bruised and broken in one of the most hostile environments on this planet. While Tillman was unable to make it out alive, a lot of people believe that Luttrell's survival was nothing short of miraculous.

Reflecting on these heroic stories, my cramps seemed irrelevant. They didn't go away, but they became nothing more than a nuisance as I made the last turn towards the finish line – the home stretch.

I was seventy-five miles from completing 26.2 miles — and I was running straight into the teeth of the wind. The wind chill had dropped to 22 degrees, and gusts reached 20 mph. It was starting to mist again.

My demons were having a party...

*"You've stopped before, you can stop again..."*
"No!"
*"What if you just walked for a little while..."*
"No!"

*"Think how disappointed you're going to be if you don't break 4 hours...."*

"Think how disappointed I'll be if I STOP?!?!?"

*"No one cares..."*

"I care!"

*"What are you trying to prove..."*

"That if I want something bad enough, I can go get it."

*"Think about all the times you've come up short in your life..."*

"Not anymore!"

As the finish line came into sight, I could see the running clock. It was past the four-hour mark — barely. It read 4:00.56.

I smiled and winked to the running gods again.

You see ... I actually started the marathon almost five minutes after everyone else. We ran into some weather on our drive to Killeen and were running a little late. The starter's pistol fired right when we arrived. I quickly checked-in, got my bib and timing chip and started running seconds after the race director said, "This is the very last call for runners."

Before I was out of earshot, I heard him say: "Turn off the music. That's it."

I was the last runner on the course.

So, with hundreds of other runners in front of me (398 to be exact), I just ran. At Mile No. 1, I started passing people and didn't stop until I had run 26.2 miles.

When I saw that clock at the finish line, I figured that I had a four- to five-minute "buffer." My chip time was all that mattered.

The clock read 4:01.51 as I crossed the finish line and the timing mat chirped. I wasn't 100 percent sure that I accomplished my goal, but I felt pretty good about it. I had given everything that I had.

Approximately thirty minutes later, I received confirmation: 3 hours, 56 minutes and 43 seconds.

I pumped my fist and smiled an exhausted smile.

On one of the coldest, dampest and windiest days that I'd EVER run, I had finally accomplished my goal. The most satisfying part, I stared down some of my most destructive demons to do it.

So, after processing everything – and finding "my words" in order to write this post – there is finally closure.

So how am I feeling?

Empowered.

I have a new sense of confidence — ready, willing and energized to tackle the next adventure. I'm excited about the next opportunity to push myself harder and further in order to accomplish something extremely important to me.

I'm already starting to ask myself...

"What's next?"

### 

## CHIGGERS, ELEPHANTS & QUESTIONABLE PARENTING?
*published March 27, 2014*

I'm a witty guy — I can come up with some pretty clever thoughts on the fly. At least that's what I thought until I had a four-year-old son.

That boy asks me some of the hardest questions in the world. They're so difficult, I can't even make up an answer.

> Crash: "What are elephants for?"
> Me: "Ummmm ... great question!"

Unfortunately, he's not looking for validation. He already knows it's a good question — that's why he asked. He wants an answer. *"What are whiskers for?" "Why did God give us skunks?" "What is an election?"*

Obviously, some of his questions have easy answers ... IF the interviewer wasn't FOUR YEARS OLD. *(Try explaining what an election is to anyone born after 2010.)*

The other day, my son asked me the mother of all questions… "What are chiggers for?"

Again, my normally witty self was completely stumped for a response. So, I excused myself to the restroom. It was time for a pep talk in the mirror.

Staring at my reflection, I berated myself…

> *"What is wrong with you?!?!?!?"*
> *"Your son wants answers!"*
> *"What ARE chiggers for?!?!?!?"*
> *"He's four years old — just say anything!"*

That last thought stopped me in my tracks. I froze, staring disappointedly at myself in the mirror.

"I can't just say anything," I whispered to myself in temporary defeat. "Now, it's elephants and chiggers – but what's he going to ask me about five years from now? Ten years from now? Thirty years from now?"

After a few seconds, I tucked my lips and nodded my head several times, acknowledging that I'd had a revelation and a possible solution.

> Crash: "Where did you go, dad?"
> Me: "To give myself a pep talk."
> Crash: "What's a pep talk for?"
> Me: "To ensure that you don't turn out to be a delinquent moron and/or an ax murderer."

While I was gathering in my thoughts in the bathroom, I realized that I don't have to have ALL the answers — whether it's about elephants and chiggers or chemistry and dating.

BUT I also realized that I couldn't stand there like a baffled deer in the headlights of an 18-wheeler, constantly muttering "great question…great question…great question."

I decided that I had two options when asked these questions:

○ Option 1 – I could answer my son's question with a question
— get his thoughts on the pressing subject at hand.

Me: "What do you think chiggers are for, Crash?"
This game plan would allow The Boy to give his creative
answer or allow us to engage in a healthy discussion
about...chiggers. (I promise...he has an answer!)

○ Option 2: I could break the news to my son that I'm actually
NOT a genius.

Me: "I don't know what chiggers are for, Brother. But we
can definitely figure it out."
This goes back to the healthy discussion from Option 1.
Nothing says father-son time like a quick Google search.

– – –

I love the fact that my son is so inquisitive. I see other adults get agitated when they get bombarded with "The Whys."

Child: "Why are we going to the grocery store?"
Adult: "To get groceries..."
Child: "Why do you need groceries?"
Adult: "Because we're out of milk, bread and fruit..."
Child: "Why are we out of those things?"
Adult: "Because we ate them..."
Child: " Why did we eat them?"
Adult: "Get. Out. Of. The. Car."

Don't get me wrong, I reach the end of my rope from time to time when the questions start flying — but I'm hoping that my new game plan turns these "interviews" into a positive experience.
The key: Perspective.

I constantly remind myself that kids are sponges, trying to soak as much in as they possibly can. They're not being malicious in any shape, form, or fashion.

My son doesn't wake up in the morning and think to himself:

> *"How can I annoy my dad today?"*
>
> *"Yesterday I asked 'why' 18 times in a row ... I wonder if I can break that record today."*
>
> *"What is the most ridiculous thing I can ask my dad about today?"*

- - -

Lastly, I wanted to put my game plan into action and share the results.

> Crash: "Do you remember that skunk that was at our house?"
> Me: "Yes, sir."
> Crash: "Me too. Why did it stink?"
> Me: "Why do you think skunks stink?"
> Crash: "Because they spray out their butts..."
> Me: "Why?"
> Crash: "To make things stinky."
> Me: "What does it smell like?"
> Crash: "Lion throw-up."
> Me *(trying not to laugh)*: "Have you ever smelled lion throw-up."
> Crash: "No, sir."
> Me: "Why haven't you smelled lion throw up?"
> Crash: "I'm tired of talking about this, daddy."

Victory!

###

## CAMPING WITH YOUR EYES WIDE OPEN
*published July 14, 2014*

B edtime comes early when you're camping with a four year old.
There are only so many marshmallows you can eat...so many games you can make up with rocks and sticks...so many mosquitoes you can fight off.

There is no late-night beer drinking around the campfire.

As the sun starts to disappear, it's usually time to call it a day. *(Especially if you're going to have enough daylight to read a bedtime story AND explain what "call it a day" means to a four year old.)*

My son and I recently ventured into the Great Outdoors for a quick two-day camping trip. It was on my current life list to take The Boy camping *(No. 37).*

If you simply want to know how the adventure turned out ... it was incredible. It was one of the most wonderfully great things that I've EVER marked off any of my lists. Words can't explain how I felt when my son said, "I like camping with you, daddy."

If you're in the mood for a little more than that ... hang on. This two-day trip completely opened my eyes and provided a life-changing reminder.

– – –

The powerful perspective of this experience hit me our first night in the tent. The sun had just disappeared beyond the horizon. The fireflies were dancing in the woods. I was WIDE awake.

"I haven't gone to bed this early since ... never," I thought to myself. I looked at my watch. It was 8:55 p.m.

So ... I traded some texts with my wife, I read a little bit of a book that I brought along, but a lot of time was spent just laying there listening to my four-year-old son saw logs like a grown man.

I decided to flip through the handful of photos that we snapped earlier in the day. There weren't a ton of pictures; we arrived at the state park around 3 o'clock, and we were busy setting up camp and exploring right up until we zipped up the tent for the night.

I was trying to document my Live the List experience, so I made a point to get out the cell phone camera at least a couple times that day.

I'm glad I did.

I don't know if it was Crash's snoring, the hot summer air blowing through the tent or the photos themselves, but I received a subtle whisper from God as I scrolled through those pics: "This is exactly where you're supposed to be."

A huge smile came across my face. I fought back tears of joy and just like any faithful man who receives validation from God ... I logged into Facebook.

I found my favorite picture from our day — a selfie we took in front of the sign for Meridian State Park – and posted it. This is the narrative that wrote to accompany it:

*I could have easily made up a dozen excuses why I shouldn't and/or couldn't take my son camping for 2 days. I could have easily kept saying, "next week" or "next month." Sometimes we have to stop lying to ourselves about how "crazy" our lives are, remember the most important things in our lives and STOP putting things off until tomorrow.*

I grabbed The Boy's hand and took a deep breath, exhaling with pure intention. The relief filled our tent. I kept thinking about the fact that we almost didn't make this trip. My Facebook status mentioned "a dozen excuses why I shouldn't and/or couldn't take my son camping."

It was more like two dozen excuses.

○    "What about my clients?"

- "What if someone wants to see a house?"
- "I have marketing deadlines coming up.
  I really need to focus on those projects."
- "Will he even remember this?"
- "I need to be writing."
- "It's going to be hot."
- "Let's wait until the fall."

This head trash was still creeping in as we drove out of the driveway for our father-son adventure.

I guess my question is … Why do we do this? Why do we talk ourselves out of doing remarkable things?

More importantly: Why do we hide our excuses behind the default response of "I'll just do it tomorrow"?

My best friend in the world is a longtime smoker. I ride his butt to quit. Throughout high school and college, it was always "I'll quit after this" or "I'll quit after that." He wanted to make it through life's twists and turns with a cigarette in his hands.

He never realized — or at least he never admitted it — there was always going to be twists and there were always going to be turns. As soon as you make it through one turn — here comes another one.

That's life!

For my buddy, "life" has kept him from putting down cigarettes for good. For the rest of us, it seems like "life" keeps a lot of us from truly living. The twists and turns keep us from doing the things we really want to do.

"After we pay off the car, THEN we will…."
"When the kids start school, THEN we will…"
"When the kids get out of school, THEN we will…"
"When I turn 40, THEN I will…."
"After I lose 25 pounds, THEN I will…"
"When I retire, THEN I will…"

When I launched my current life list, I wrote about this tragedy. It's worth repeating:

The worst phrase in the English language is "I'll do it tomorrow."

Those four and half words are dream killers, and I firmly believe that they are the primary reason people don't accomplish their goals and fall short of their aspirations. That phrase paralyzes us to do nothing and embrace the status quo (*bored, joyless, unhappy, uninspired, lost*).

Instead of attacking life and going after what we really want, we fall into the same-ol' same-ol' — foolishly confident that there will be a tomorrow. If we knew the exact day we were going to die, we could throw around the phrase "I'll do it tomorrow" with 100 percent certainty.

We don't.

Tomorrow is nothing more than a hope.

The philosopher Eminem said it best: "The truth is you don't know what is going to happen tomorrow. Life is a crazy ride, and nothing is guaranteed."

– – –

As I laid there in our tent, holding my son's hand, I thought about the other facets of my life that are impacted by foolish excuses. What else in my life is being affected by the reckless and arrogant phrase "I'll do it tomorrow"?

Well….

I have three life lists with a number of unaccomplished dreams and aspirations…

I have a handful of book ideas dancing around in my head…

I have countless life lessons that I haven't taught my kids yet…

I'm still holding stupid grudges….

Nike told us to "Just Do It." Were they only talking about the things we do while we're wearing their sneakers? I really don't think they were.

We need to draw a line in the sand and DO IT.

We need to stop making up lame excuses and DO IT.

We need to stop lying to ourselves and DO IT.

Question: What is "IT?"

Answer: Whatever the hell is important to YOU. Whatever the hell is important to ME.

It might be a simple life list thing — learn to play the guitar, eat sushi, take your son camping, OR it might be a game-changing thing — finally telling someone that you love them or forgiving someone.

If you're naïve … er … stupid enough to think that tomorrow is a guarantee, you deserve to die with regrets.

Ask Richard Durrett, the beloved writer for ESPN.com who covered the Rangers, Cowboys and Stars, if he planned on dying from an aneurysm at the age of thirty-eight. Since his wife was expecting their third child at the time of his death — I'm guessing he didn't.

No tomorrow.

Ask *Fast and Furious* star Paul Walker, who died in a senseless car wreck while he was out joyriding at the age of forty.

No tomorrow.

You *know* that I could go on and on with countless number stories like this. The news articles and obituaries tie all of these tragedies together with two simple words: "died unexpectedly."

No tomorrow.

– – –

Even though my mind was racing in the warm tent that night, I felt a sense of clarity and peace come over me. Fatigue set in next. I looked at my watch again. It was just before 11 o'clock.

I decided to try and sleep.

As I closed my eyes, I grabbed The Boy's hand again and whispered aloud: "Thank you, God."

###

## TAKE YOUR 'REAL JOB' AND SHOVE IT
*published March 2, 2015*

I don't ask questions on Facebook. It's not my thing.
I guess I get it...

- "Visiting Miami...does anyone know a good restaurant on South Beach?"
- "Looking for a book to read on my cruise...any suggestions?"
- "Thinking about getting a tattoo...should I get the pig with a snake in its mouth?"
- "Where should I get the before-mentioned tattoo?"

Again, it's not my thing.

I slipped the other day when I wrote a fun, light-hearted status update. It said:

I recently submitted a résumé that forced me to self-brand myself all in the name of #livethelist. My newly generated job title: "Enlivener" — a person who restores *(something)* to life, gives life to *(something)*; a person who makes *(something)* more entertaining, interesting, or appealing.

Then, I broke my personal policy on begging for comments by writing: "Thoughts?"

In all honesty... it was a rhetorical question — I knew my made-up title was wonderfully great – but I guess the tone was lost in cyberspace.

To my surprise, however, I received some interesting feedback.

"Dig."

"Describes you..."

"For almost any other person, I'd be cynical and skeptical. You, on the other hand..."

Again, I wasn't looking for validation, but there were some nice comments. Then there were a handful of "friends" who saw a prime opportunity to fire a shot across my bow.

Before I go down that road, though … here is a little back-story about my self-branding post.

I was recently approved to teach a Live the List continuing education class at Tarleton State University this summer and next fall. As part of the process, the university needed me to submit a résumé.

I had no problem laying out my eleven jobs in eleven years after college … BUT I had to find my résumé. For the life of me, I couldn't remember the last time that I submitted one to a potential "employer."

When I started selling real estate – NO résumé needed.

When I launched my marketing and communications company – NO résumé needed.

When I became a part-time stay-at-home dad – NO résumé needed.

I finally found it, and then it was time to dust it off.

Since I was applying for a "job" that revolved around my Live the List Project, I didn't think being a real estate agent was going to get me the job. After a lot of brainstorming, I decided to give myself a fancy title for all the hard work that I've put into Live the List.

Enlivener!

I had to come up with something – an umbrella that covered the following duties:

- Developing a unique platform around Live the List Project, which puts people's goals, dreams and aspirations in the Spotlight
- Writing a regular blog and a book about Live the List Project
- Speaking to civic groups, churches and non-profit organizations about Live the List Project
- Coordinating the launch of a Live the List radio show I thought "Enlivener" was PERFECT. Again, it was 100 percent bullshit – BUT it got my point across and helped get me the job.

Sooooo … about those comments on Facebook.

After re-reading all of them – I realized that they were mostly all in good fun. Just a little ribbing from family and friends. *(e.g. "What's the pay scale on that profession??!")*

But there was ONE comment that stuck with me. It poetically said: "I think you should get a real job. You asked … and it would be a nice thing to check off 'the list.' "

My initial response was a gigantic smile. *(Not sure why.)*

Then I felt a surge of inspiration. I whispered to myself: "I'll show you 'real job' when all of this hard work pays off."

Then I asked the universe the million-dollar question: What the hell is a "real job?"

Then the follow-up questions started flowing:

- Do I have to work at least 40 to 60 hours a week for it to be a "real job?"
- Do I have to constantly bitch about what I do for a living for it to be a "real job?"
- Do I have to do meaningless tasks to help someone else make a buck for it to be a "real job?"
- Do I have to dread going to work on Monday morning for it to be a "real job?"
- Do I have to count the days until the weekend for it to be a "real job?"
- Do I have to count the years until I can retire and THEN do what I really want to do with my life? Does THAT make it a "real job?"

"Real jobs" are just as much bullshit as my made-up title. AND I won't be getting a "real job" anytime soon.

###

# CLIMBING THE MOUNTAIN OF PROCRASTINATION
*published July 22, 2015*

Two thousand, five hundred and twenty-nine.

That's exactly how many days "Summiting a Fourteener" was on my life list before I stopped making bullshit excuses and FINALLY marked it off. Climbing a 14,000-foot mountain was No. 15 on the first life list that I ever created in 2008, and it had been on every life list since. *(That's a total of four life lists if you're keeping track of how pathetic it is.)*

For almost seven years, I made up one reason after another why it wasn't the right time to mark this lofty task off my list. *(I won't bore you with all the excuses, but they were ludicrous – especially since I fly for free and I have family in Colorado.)*

If it's not completely obvious...I'm beyond embarrassed to admit this out loud. I was constantly encouraging people – practically preaching to them – to stop saying, "I'll do it tomorrow" and pull the trigger on their goals, dreams and aspirations.

The whole time, I had my thumb inserted into my hypocritical butt.

I was talking the talk, but I definitely wasn't walking the walk.

I was just another jerk who ignorantly believed that there would be a tomorrow. I was being a naïve fool who assumed there would be another summer to accomplish this goal.

So. Embarrassing. *(Not to mention tragic.)*

When I created my most recent Life List – fifty-five new things that I wanted to accomplish over the next 555 days – I put "Summit a Four-teener" on there AGAIN. It was No. 16 this time around.

Around this same time, I was getting ready to teach my Live the List continuing education classes *(another Life List item)*. One of the discussion items that I had planned for the class revolved around taking action.

The question: "What makes us finally say 'Screw it...I'm going to pull the trigger and do it?' No. More. Excuses."

No one – including myself – had a solid answer. The discussion was generic at best.

Then I tweaked the question just a little and asked my students: "Instead of trying to figure out what motivates us to finally take action ... what keeps us from pulling the trigger in the first place? What keeps us from going for it?"

And just for the record ... "it" could be anything. It could be learning to sew, telling that special someone that you love them OR climbing a 14,000-foot mountain.

Once I framed the question like this, the discussion took off.

A lot of the answers revolved around time, money and fear, but the answer that intrigued me the most had to do with the metaphorical "hamster wheel" of life.

One of my students said: "The hamster wheel is easy. You know what to expect. There are no surprises. If you get off the hamster wheel and do something out of the ordinary, there is a possibility it could throw off your whole week."

I asked for an example.

"A friend asked me to go out to dinner the other night, and I said no. It had nothing to do with prior obligations or the fact I didn't want to see my friend. It had everything to do with how it was going to impact the next day and possibly the day after that.

"I knew I'd get to bed late, and I'd be tired the whole next day. I knew I wouldn't want to get up and go to the gym, so I'd have to go after work – if I went at all. If I did talk myself into going to the gym after work, I'd miss my favorite TV show. I thought about just recording it and watching it later, but that would mean going to bed late two nights in a row and...."

She abruptly stopped her example and said: "It's just easier to do the same ol' same ol'."

Some people in the class tucked their lips and gave her a "you're absolutely right" nod. Others stared blankly at the desk in front of them, a little embarrassed because she had just described them.

I chose to tuck my lips and nod. She had nailed it.

That night, I went home and made my plane reservation to Colorado.

"If this really is important to you, you'll stop making excuses and do it," I whispered to myself.

We left Denver at 5 a.m. and drove towards the dark purple mountains on the horizon. My cousin, a Colorado native, had agreed to climb a 14,000-foot peak with me and help me mark No. 16 off my Live the List. He had done his first and only fourteener with his wife the summer before. Compared to this Texas boy, he was an expert.

After a lot of discussion, we decided to bag two fourteeners on the same day – Grays Peak and Torreys Peak. They were adjacent to each other, with only a narrow saddleback connecting the two peaks.

As we parked the truck and entered the trailhead, both peaks loomed in the distance. I wasn't intimated, though. Yes, they were impressive, but not bullying.

I was a little naïve.

As we got closer and closer to the base of the mountain – after a 1.5-mile hike through a scenic valley – I could start to see people slowly working their way up the side of the mountain. They looked like lethargic carpenter ants, working back and forth across the grade.

The higher I gazed up the rocky slope, the smaller the people looked and the slower they were moving. I kept thinking to myself: "I'm about to be up there!"

Now, I was officially intimated, but I kept putting one foot in front of the other.

At one point of the climb, I started counting my steps and then stopping to catch my breath and allow my legs to stop screaming. My cousin's wife said I would have to do this, but I thought she was messing with me.

Nope!

At first, I'd take seventy-five steps and stop for ten or fifteen seconds.

Then, I'd take sixty steps at a time and then rest for twenty seconds.

Fifty steps.

Forty steps.

As I approached the second summit, I was only taking 30 steps before stopping for thirty seconds. The incline was steep, the air was thin, and my legs felt like grape jelly. I was being slow and intentional moving up this rocky incline.

Confession: I didn't have a choice. If I wanted to accomplish this goal, I was going to do it 30 steps at a time.

A lot of people have asked me: "Was it hard?"

I'm always quick to say "yes," but I also say, "It was never undoable." I told one friend: "I never thought to myself, 'I can't do this.'"

There was one instance when I slightly questioned what I was doing, but that self-doubt was short-lived. It was after we bagged our first peak, Grays, and I convinced my cousin to tackle Torreys Peak as well.

As we descended from the top of Grays and onto the saddleback that connected the two peaks, that's when I whispered to myself: "Maybe this wasn't a good idea." The wind was blowing hard. It was cold. My legs were fatigued.

But then I said out loud: "Keep going!"

I'm so glad that I did.

Torreys Peak was perfect. The wind had subsided. The sun had warmed up the cool air. The view was indescribable. But it was the sense of accomplishment that was so satisfying. There were a lot of people on that mountain with us, but there were millions that wouldn't even have attempted what we just did.

Standing on top of that 14,274-foot mountain, I felt alive. I felt bullet proof. I felt like I could accomplish anything in the world.

When I did my hut-to-hut bike ride in Colorado a few years before, I wrote this narrative: "I was pushing my body harder and longer than I ever thought possible; I was in the middle of some of the most beautiful country in the world, and I didn't know what was going to be thrown at me next – a true adventure!"

That is exactly how I felt on top of that mountain.

– – –

On the descent, my mind was going 100 mph. I kept asking myself: "Why did I wait so long to do this? Why did I keep putting this off? Why did I keep saying 'I'll do it tomorrow?'"

I didn't have a solid answer.

Then I thought about all the other tasks that have cemented themselves on my life lists – never getting marked off for one reason or another.

Some examples:

- Take a martial arts class
- Zip line
- Get a tattoo
- Visit the Grand Canyon

Then I whispered that defining phrase that finally made me pull the trigger on my 14,000-foot adventure. "If these things are really important to you, you'll stop making excuses and do them!"

When we got back to the trailhead – sore and battered, but feeling euphoric – there was only one more question looming: "Which one of these tasks is next?!?!?"

###

# *Acknowledgments*

In Chapter 13, I shared the concept of relational joy. I was introduced to this term by a spiritual mentor of mine *(shout out Rev. Ken Horton)*. I instantly fell in love with it. Like I mentioned in the book, relational joy focuses on laying up eternal treasures in heaven, and those treasures revolve around the people we spiritually touch during our lifetime.

I have been so blessed, because my life has been positively impacted by so many wonderfully great people. Throughout the book, I gave specific shout outs to certain individuals, but there are so many more people who I need to recognize.

Make the important things important, right? Expressing my love and gratitude to the following individuals was *very* important to me.

Thanks to my family – especially my wife, my kids and my sisters – for letting me be extra.

Thanks to my Mom and Dad for loving me even when that was hard to do.

Thanks to my cousin, Brent Walters, who walked the walk as a man and showed me how to do the same.

Thanks to my cousin, Mary Collier, for pushing to make myself a priority.

Thanks to Mike and Scott for loving my sisters.

Thanks to all my friends. So many friends.

Thanks to Nick Eatman for always being my biggest advocate and never letting me forget the funniest parts of the journey.

Thanks to Greg Jones, who has been there since Mrs. Gilmer's fifth-grade class; and thanks to Greg for not walking away when I shot him with a BB gun in junior high.

Thanks to Chris Gilliand for heading west with me on that ultimate adventure to Oregon.

Thanks to Brad, Hatton and Tomas.

Thanks to Dave and Kimbra.

Thanks to Kelly Imig and Alex Cunningham for never forgetting my birthday.

Thanks to Melanie Hanna for giving me the opportunity to meet Pudge Rodriguez, my all-time favorite baseball player.

Thanks to Shauna Glenn for reminding me how much I like to laugh.

Thanks to Dennisha Denney for wrapping her arms around my inspirational message and pushing me to play big.

Thanks to all my bosses who made those eleven jobs in eleven years a fantastic adventure – Barbara Merkle, Mike Sinquefield, and Bill Vineyard.

Thanks to Everett Todd and Scott Maxfield for giving me a chance to chase my crazy dream of coaching football.

Thanks to Julie and Mike Greene for single-handedly changing the trajectory of my life when they started a radio station in Glen Rose, Texas.

Thanks to Michael White for letting me keep my radio dream alive.

Thanks to Gloria Moncrief Holmsten and The Saving Hope Foundation for helping me fund the adventure for all those years.

Thanks to all my family and friends – and even the strangers – who pledged to my Kickstarter campaign in order to make this book a reality.

Thanks to my author friends – Lou Redmond and Chelsea Hooper – who unknowingly blazed the trail and inspired me to finish this book.

Thanks to author Kristen Ethridge for her incredible advice and guidance.

Thanks to my beta readers, especially Joy – the best writer that I've ever known.

Thanks to my new friends – Bonnie, Mandie, and Melanie – who brought *Tacos and Chocolate* to life.

Here is some random appreciation:

Thanks to all my investors in e-Partners in Giving; it is my shadow mission in life to repay you guys for believing in my wild and crazy entrepreneurial idea.

Thanks to Drew Kennedy and Lori McKenna for writing *Rose of Jericho*; that song gives me peace – and confidence – when I'm juggling balloons in the eye of the chaos.

Thanks to author Steve Farber for introducing me to the concept of "love-inspired audacity;" that was a game-changer in my life.

Finally, thanks to Tommy Arens for letting me borrow his truck in the summer of 1994 after my 1971 Chevy died on the side of the road in Wichita Falls, Texas. *(I always said that I was going to give him some serious love for that selfless act of kindness!)*

# Sources

Rura, Nicole. Harvard School of Public Health. Close to half of U.S. population projected to have obesity by 2030. https://www.hsph.harvard.edu/news/press-releases/half-of-us-to-have-obesity-by-2030/.

Mandino, Og. *The Greatest Miracle in the World*. Reissue edition. Bantam, 1983. (Chapter 9)

Maraniss, David. *When Pride Still Mattered: A Life of Vince Lombardi*. Touchstone, 2000.

Hill, Napoleon. *Think and Grow Rich: Instant Aid to Riches*. Hawthorn Books, Inc, 1966.

Byrne, Rhonda. *The Secret*. Atria Books/Beyond Words, 2006.

Myers, Drew. *Defining Audacity. Ever Had To Clean-Up Puke? I Almost Did!. https://definingaudacity.wordpress.com/2009/05/07/ever-had-to-cleanup-puke-i-almost-did/*

Ferriss, Timothy. *The 4-Hour Workweek*. Crown Publishers, 2007. (252-253)

Day Zero Project. https://dayzeroproject.com

Guillebeau, Chris. *The Art of Non-Conformity: Set Your Own Rules, Live the Life You Want, and Change the World*. Perigee. January 2010.

McRaven, Admiral William H. *Make Your Bed.* Grand Central Publishing, 2017. (93-94)

Krakauer, Jon. *Into the Wild.* Anchor Books, 1997.

Farber, Steve. *The Radical Leap: A Personal Lesson in Extreme Leadership.* Kaplan Publishing, 2009.

Myers, Drew. *Defining Audacity.* The Ultimate Goal: Seeing Your Kids Shine. December 2014. https://definingaudacity.wordpress.com/2014/12/01/ultimategoal/

Myers, Drew. *Defining Audacity.* An Empowering Look in the Mirror. May 2020. https://definingaudacity.wordpress.com/2020/05/29/an-empowering-look-in-the-mirror/

Kravitz, Len, Ph.D. The University of New Mexico. Exercise Motivation: What Starts and Keeps People Exercising? 2011. https://www.unm.edu/~lkravitz/Article%20folder/ExerciseMot.pdf

McLeod, Dr. Saul. *Simply Psychology.* Maslow's Hierarchy of Needs. December 2020. https://www.simplypsychology.org/maslow.html

Tech Jury. How Much Time Do People Spend on Social Media in 2021? August 2021. https://techjury.net/blog/time-spent-on-social-media/#gref

Myers, Drew. *Defining Audacity.* 1,000 Days of Running: Streaking Out of the Spotlight. November 2013. https://definingaudacity.wordpress.com/2013/11/04/runningmilestone/

Albom, Mitch. *Have a Little Faith: A True Story.* Reprint edition. Hachette Books, 2011.

Kelly, Matthew. *The Rhythm of Life: Living Every Day with Passion & Purpose*. 3rd edition. Blue Sparrow, 2015.

Roy, Sandip. Facebook Envy: 7 Sad Facts (And 4 Strategies To Stop It). https://happyproject.in/facebook-envy/

Kelly, Heather. CNN Business. Study: Using Facebook Can Make You Sad. 2013. https://www.cnn.com/2013/08/15/tech/social-media/study-facebook-blues/index.html

Wiley, Elizabeth. King 5 News. Survey finds 56% of people use Facebook on the toilet. https://www.krem.com/article/tech/survey-finds-56-of-people-use-facebook-on-the-toilet/293-287970803

Deyan G. *Tech Survey*. How Much Time Do People Spend on Social Media in 2021? August, 2021.

Bauder, David. ABC News. Study shows explosive growth in time spent streaming TV. February 2020. https://abcnews.go.com/Lifestyle/wireStory/study-shows-explosive-growth-time-spent-streaming-tv-68940265

Department of Health and Human Services. Strategic Goal 2: Protect the Health of Americans Where They Live, Learn, Work, and Play. April 2020. https://www.hhs.gov/about/strategic-plan/strategic-goal-2/index.html

Perrin, Andrew. Pew Research Center. Who doesn't read books in America? September 2019. https://www.pewresearch.org/fact-tank/2019/09/26/who-doesnt-read-books-in-america/

Sifferlin, Alexandra. *Time*. Here's How Happy Americans Are Right Now. July 2017. https://time.com/4871720/how-happy-are-americans/

Elrod, Hal. *The Miracle Morning.* Hal Elrod International, Inc. 2016. (49-52)

Robbins, Mel. *The Five Elements of the 5 Second Rule.* April 2018. https://melrobbins.com/five-elements-5-second-rule/

National Alliance to End Homelessness. State of Homelessness: 2021 Edition. https://endhomelessness.org/homelessness-in-america/home-lessness-statistics/state-of-homelessness-2021/

Action Against Hunger. World Hunger: Key Facts and Statistics 2021. https://www.actionagainsthunger.org/world-hunger-facts-statistics

Adopt US Kids. About the children. https://www.adoptuskids.org/meet-the-children/children-in-foster-care/about-the-children

Smith, Alex. *The Cares Family.* TV is not the answer to loneliness, but it can help build connection in disconnecting times. July 2020. https://www.thecaresfamily.org.uk/blog/tv-is-not-the-answer-to-loneli-ness-but-it-can-help-build-connection-in-disconnecting-times

Diemart, Rui. *One Young World.* 32 million American adults can't read: why literacy is the key to growth. February 2018. https://medium.com/@OneYoungWorld_/32-million-american-adults-cant-read-why-literacy-is-the-key-to-growth-818996739523

Ross, Jenna. *Visual Capitalist.* How Many People Die Each Day? May 2020. https://www.visualcapitalist.com/how-many-people-die-each-day/

American Cancer Society. Cancer Facts & Figures 2020. 2020. https://www.cancer.org/research/cancer-facts-statistics/all-cancer-facts-figures/cancer-facts-figures-2020.html

Andrews, Andy. *The Noticer Returns: Sometimes You Find Perspective, and Sometimes Perspective Finds You.* Thomas Nelson, 2013.

Miller, Donald. *Building a StoryBrand: Seven proven elements of powerful stories.* Generic, 2018.

Buffini, Brain. *The Brian Buffini Show.* Flexibility Equals Freedom. October 2020.

Lucado, Max. *Fearless.* Thomas Nelson, 2012.

Weingarten, Gene. *The Washington Post.* Pearls Before Breakfast: Can one of the nation's great musicians cut through the fog of a D.C. rush hour? Let's find out. April 2007. https://www.washingtonpost.com/lifestyle/magazine/pearls-before-breakfast-can-one-of-the-nations-great-musicians-cut-through-the-fog-of-a-dc-rush-hour-lets-find-out/2014/09/23/8a6d46da-4331-11e4-b47c-f5889e061e5f_story.html

Celiac Disease Foundation. What is Gluten? https://celiac.org/gluten-free-living/what-is-gluten/

American Heart Association. Carbohydrates. April 2018. https://www.heart.org/en/healthy-living/healthy-eating/eat-smart/nutrition-basics/carbohydrates

Myers, Drew. *Defining Audacity.* Defining an Adventure. May 2008. https://definingaudacity.wordpress.com/2008/05/03/adventure/

Myers, Drew. *Defining Audacity.* Defining Moment: What is the Real Meaning of 'DNF'? April 2009. https://definingaudacity.wordpress.com/2009/04/27/defining-moment-what-is-real-meaning-of-dnf/

Myers, Drew. *Defining Audacity*. A Fabulous Farewell ... to ME! June 2012.        https://definingaudacity.wordpress.com/2012/06/06/funeralarrangements/

Myers, Drew. *Defining Audacity*. My Dirty Little Secret...Blogging Greatness? June 2012. https://definingaudacity.wordpress.com/2012/06/15/dirtylittlesecret/

Myers, Drew. *Defining Audacity*. Getting Physical With Perfection. October 2013. https://definingaudacity.wordpress.com/2013/10/08/gettingphysical/

Myers, Drew. *Defining Audacity*. Fight to the Finish: Demons Can't Stop Historic Run. March 2014. https://definingaudacity.wordpress.com/2014/03/04/armymarathon/

Myers, Drew. *Defining Audacity*. Chiggers, Elephants & Questionable Parenting? March 2014. https://definingaudacity.wordpress.com/2014/05/27/questionableparenting/

Myers, Drew. *Defining Audacity*. Camping With Your Eyes Wide Open. July 2014. https://definingaudacity.wordpress.com/2014/07/14/summercamp/

Myers, Drew. *Defining Audacity*. Take Your 'Real Job' and Shove It. March 2015. https://definingaudacity.wordpress.com/2015/03/02/realjob/

Myers, Drew. *Defining Audacity*. Climbing the Mountain of Procrastination. July 2015. https://definingaudacity.wordpress.com/2015/07/22/climbing-the-mountain-of-procrastination/

CPSIA information can be obtained
at www.ICGtesting.com
Printed in the USA
LVHW020153290921
698984LV00002B/154

9 781943 377121